Better Homes and Gardens®

Kitchen
Idea File

Better Homes and Gardens® Books
Des Moines, Iowa

Better Homes and Gardens® Books
An imprint of Meredith® Books

Kitchen Idea File
Editor: Amy Tincher-Durik
Contributing Editors: Cynthia Pearson, Dan Weeks
Art Director: David Jordan
Copy Chief: Terri Fredrickson
Copy and Production Editor: Victoria Forlini
Editorial Operations Manager: Karen Schirm
Managers, Book Production: Pam Kvitne, Marjorie J. Schenkelberg, Rick von Holdt
Contributing Copy Editor: Kim Catanzarite
Contributing Proofreaders: Becky Etchen, Sue Fetters, Brenda Scott Royce
Contributing Illustrator: Tom Stocki
Contributing Stylist: Becky Jerdee
Indexer: Elizabeth Parson
Electronic Production Coordinator: Paula Forest
Editorial and Design Assistants: Kaye Chabot, Karen McFadden, Mary Lee Gavin

Meredith® Books
Editor in Chief: Linda Raglan Cunningham
Design Director: Matt Strelecki
Executive Editor, Home Decorating and Design: Denise L. Caringer

Publisher: James D. Blume
Executive Director, Marketing: Jeffrey Myers
Executive Director, New Business Development: Todd M. Davis
Executive Director, Sales: Ken Zagor
Director, Operations: George A. Susral
Director, Production: Douglas M. Johnston
Business Director: Jim Leonard

Vice President and General Manager: Douglas J. Guendel

Better Homes and Gardens® **Magazine**
Editor in Chief: Karol DeWulf Nickell

Meredith Publishing Group
President, Publishing Group: Stephen M. Lacy
Vice President-Publishing Director: Bob Mate

Meredith Corporation
Chairman and Chief Executive Officer: William T. Kerr

Chairman of the Executive Committee: E. T. Meredith III

All of us at Better Homes and Gardens® Books are dedicated to providing you with information and ideas to enhance your home. We welcome your comments and suggestions. Write to us at: Better Homes and Gardens Books, Home Decorating and Design Editorial Department, 1716 Locust St., Des Moines, IA 50309-3023.

If you would like to purchase any of our home decorating and design, cooking, crafts, gardening, or home improvement books, check wherever quality books are sold. Or visit us at: bhgbooks.com

Cover Photograph: Jon Jensen

Inspiring Case Studies to Plan Your Kitchen Design

In your hands you hold the key to building or remodeling your dream kitchen: *Better Homes and Gardens® Kitchen Idea File*. This inspirational book combines kitchen case studies with tips and strategies to help you customize your kitchen to perfectly suit your needs and lifestyle. Chapter 1, ***Review***, includes a variety of typical kitchen problems and real-life, ingenious solutions to those problems. The chapters that follow introduce a variety of strategies by way of informational tips and Idea File sections that give the lowdown on the latest techniques. Chapter 2 shows how to ***Refresh*** worn or dated kitchens that are otherwise functional with simple facelifts that provide maximum impact at a minimal cost. Chapter 3 illustrates diverse ways to ***Remodel*** a kitchen that has structural or organizational problems. Chapter 4, ***Make New***, shows what you can achieve by starting from scratch when building a kitchen in a new home or gutted space. Looking for ideas for mudrooms and laundries? You'll find great ideas in Chapter 5, ***Rooms Around the Kitchen***. ***Kitchen Elements***, Chapter 6, introduces the latest problem-solving kitchen products and materials. Finally, Chapter 7, ***Strategies & Resources***, helps you transform all of your ideas together into a plan for your new kitchen, with tips on communicating with the professionals and overviews on products that you'll need to make your dream kitchen a reality. Are you ready?

Is your kitchen ready for a change? Perhaps the cooks keep bumping into one another because the layout is inefficient. Or maybe you'd like to add a breakfast nook or a snack bar. Do you need more counter or storage space, or do you want to open the room to an adjoining living, dining, or family room? If you entertain often, you may want to create an in-kitchen gathering area. No matter what your situation, you'll find a solution that's right for you.

See page 15

See page 25

This chapter provides a quick review of many kitchens, from small to large, and some that are specialized. They've been remodeled or built from scratch to suit their owners' needs, and they're packed with ideas you can apply to your own kitchen project. Whether you are considering a simple update—with fresh colors and accessories—or a substantial kitchen remodeling or addition, look here first for ideas to jump-start your planning process.

Review

Mini-Kitchen
Turns Terrific

1

A very small kitchen in a Portland, Oregon, house desperately needed a redo. At only 7 feet wide, it lacked storage space and sufficient work areas; bumping elbows was unavoidable when one person worked at the sink and another at the stove. What makes this addition so successful is that it respects—and even enhances—the style of the original house, both inside and out. It also adds enough square footage to allow a roomy work core and a large island that straddles old and new spaces. Now there's plenty of room to cook, gather, and entertain.

2

SITUATION

- The kitchen was so small that large meals were prepared in shifts, then reheated.
- Storage and counter space was minimal.
- The traffic routes were awful: The hallway-size kitchen is also the only route from the mudroom—the most-used entry—to the rest of the house.
- The Cape Cod architecture could lose its charm to an ill-conceived or out-of-scale addition.
- Lovely mature trees in the backyard would be sacrificed if a conventional addition were built.

SOLUTIONS

- Build an 8×16-foot addition with enough room for a spacious work core.
- Narrow the doorway into the mudroom for more counter and storage space.
- Move the work core out of the traffic pattern for increased efficiency.
- Complement the scale, style, and detailing of the original house.
- Preserve trees with careful planning.

MUDROOM KITCHEN

Before

MUDROOM KITCHEN NOOK DINING DECK PATIO

After

Tree-Preserving *Tips*

Most likely you can have your addition and keep your trees too. Ask a site-conscious architect, designer, or contractor how you can work your new space around established trees. Often a solution includes the use of pier footings (individual blocks of concrete) beneath a foundation rather than using continuous concrete. Typically pier footings offer some flexibility in where they are located beneath the slab so they result in much less disruption of tree roots. Such footings preserve trees that might otherwise die, as traditional foundation digging may sever, damage, or compact the soil around too many tree roots. With any type of footing, it's important to work carefully. Heavy equipment that compacts the soil around roots, digs holes larger than necessary, or bangs up the tree trunk and scrapes off bark (which carries water and nutrients throughout the tree) may damage or kill trees. Hand digging; using new, smaller, lighter excavation equipment; and careful operating can make the difference between a tree that thrives and one that dies.

3
4

1 *A butcher-block island provides plenty of work space. This island's vintage styling and furniture details complement an antique sideboard that resides in the kitchen. Cabinets made of pine from an old church organ and a beaded-board backsplash harmonize with the home's original cottage look.*

2 *A gabled dormer and windows with muntins visually connect the addition to the rest of the house. A covered deck expands the kitchen's capacity, serving as an outdoor living and dining space, even in misty weather.*

3 *A compact, yet powerful, range shows that commercial equipment won't necessarily dominate the look or the space of a modest-size, country-style kitchen.*

4 *This nook was custom made for the family-heirloom buffet. Cabinetry above helps tie the antique buffet to the rest of the kitchen.*

Charm Meets Efficiency

COTTAGE

The kitchen in a 1920s cottage on Delaware's Rehoboth Beach had vintage charm but was short on storage space and difficult to work in. A moderate-size remodeling project blends existing elements from the cottage with new elements to preserve the room's nostalgic feel while boosting its efficiency. The original layout remains intact.

SITUATION

- The kitchen lacks a unifying focal point.
- The room is boxed-in and isolated.
- The windows are low, leaving little room for standard-height cabinets, a counter, and storage space.
- A place is needed to compose grocery lists, write notes, and take messages.

SOLUTIONS

- Import a vintage console sink from the mudroom to boost the kitchen's nostalgic ambience and create a focal point.
- Replace a full wall that separates the kitchen and dining room with a half-wall.
- Reposition the windows higher on the wall, making room for cabinets and a counter.
- Install a small built-in desk.

3

4

1 New cabinets, some painted white and some left natural, blend with the original cupboards and a vintage sink in this beach-cottage kitchen. The cabinets match the floor, ceiling, white walls, and appliances. The original floor is refinished; the ceiling is left natural.

2 A shallow plate rack offers an attractive display and storage solution over the cooktop. The copper back of the rack's shelf matches antique lights hanging over the sink.

3 A half-wall replaces a full one, visually opening the kitchen and dining room spaces to each other.

4 A desk surface slipped beneath a window and between some cabinets creates a handy spot to sit and jot down grocery lists and take care of correspondence.

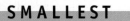

Tall
Order

SMALLEST

The order was for more light, an efficient work space, 1920s style, and a better view. With the help of a couple of modest yet well-designed bump-outs, this 11×12-foot space is proof that you don't have to spend a lot of money or add a lot of space to make a dramatic difference in the way a small kitchen looks, works, and feels.

Before

After

- The kitchen is oppressively dark; little natural light permeates the space.
- One window looks onto an unattractive view of the neighbor's garage.
- The layout is inefficient; the refrigerator and sink are too far apart.
- There's no place to eat a meal, do paperwork, or sort mail.

- Add a triangle-shape bump-out with a glazed door and tall window to gather lots of light and show off a pretty view.
- Build another bump-out—just the width of a kitchen counter—for a peninsula with a sink and dishwasher.
- Back the peninsula with a bar-height counter and some stools.
- Run a narrow desk with overhead cubicles along the wall behind the peninsula.

1 Butcher block, beaded board, and naturally finished floors and cabinets contribute to the vintage feel of a 1920s kitchen.

2 A granite countertop and stainless appliances add a commercial edge to the otherwise countrylike space.

3 A desk and pair of tall cabinets create a transition between the kitchen and the dining room. A shelf holds favorite cookbooks; pigeonholes corral bills, CDs, and other small items.

4 Every sliver of this remodeled kitchen is put to work: A 3-inch-deep space at the end of the peninsula houses a set of spice shelves.

13

A Step

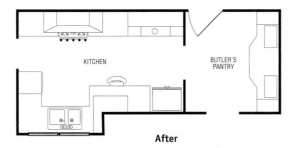

KITCHEN

BUTLER'S PANTRY

After

SMALL

If there's no room for your small kitchen to grow, you can still expand its function and feel by looking high and low for more space and creating the illusion of more room than exists. Doing so requires a good eye, much forethought, and careful measuring to make sure everything not only looks right but fits well. This 126-square-foot kitchen in a 1920s home is a great example of the drama that results from careful, artful planning and execution.

SITUATION

- The kitchen lacks storage space.
- The existing cabinet space is inefficient for pots and pans.
- The galley layout makes the kitchen look even smaller than it is.
- There's no place to display plants, books, and personal objects.
- A desk space is needed.

SOLUTIONS

- Eliminate some upper cabinets—and make the room seem more spacious—by adding storage to an adjoining butler's pantry.
- Install a hanging rail and hooks for storing pots and pans, thereby freeing more room in the cupboards for other items.
- Create visual excitement by varying cabinet heights and adding decorative elements, such as floor tiles that mix shiny and matte finishes.
- Leave some storage spaces open to view, such as those beneath the countertops and above the wall ovens, allowing the eye to take in the texture and detail of what's stored or displayed there.
- Place a kneehole and stool beneath the countertop, effectively adding a desk without intruding on the room's space.

1 Open shelving mixes storage with display—and makes cookware easy to get at. Glass sides help reduce the visual volume of the hood over the commercial range.

2 A pot rack puts cookware on display, freeing cabinets for other uses. Artful finishes on the walls and floors add texture and visual interest.

3 Varying the depth and height of cabinets helps create visual excitement in a small space. A kneehole and stool efficiently turn a section of countertop into a desk.

4 A pullout pantry means all items are within convenient reach, even in a deep cabinet.

Whiten &
Brighten

GALLEY

Even with a skylight and sliding door added in an earlier renovation, this galley kitchen remained dark. Dingy wood cabinets and black appliances seemed to suck the light from the room. With randomly placed appliances interrupting the countertops, the kitchen wasn't all that functional either. The room's redesign stays within the existing walls but brightens and streamlines both the look and function of what's now a great little galley.

- The kitchen felt dark and cavelike.
- The back entry to the kitchen was drafty, because of an awkward sliding glass door.
- Appliance placement cut countertop runs into short, useless pieces.

SOLUTIONS

- Maximize window light by switching to all-white cabinetry and appliances.
- Replace the sliding glass door with a more gracious-looking, easier-opening, efficient French door.
- Group appliances on one side of the kitchen, leaving a broad length of counter-top on the other side.

1 White cabinets and appliances streamline the appliance wall. Natural-finish hardwood floors add visual warmth. A planning area at one end of the kitchen takes advantage of natural light there.

2 The muntin grid on the hutch's glass doors mimics those on the adjacent French door. The use of glass helps the kitchen feel more expansive. Operable sidelights let in fresh air.

3 Melon-color solid-surface counter-tops balance the white cabinets and backsplash theme.

Big Family, Big Cooking

MULTI-COOK

How do you make room for 600 tomatoes and five or more cooks and helpers? An expansive island surface holds a large family's garden bounty, while multiple work-stations host an abundance of cooks. When everyone's chopping and cooking, this kitchen hums with effi-ciency. Pullouts reign here, from the spice cabinet and drawers situated inside the base cabinets to hidden cutting boards that make good use of the narrowest of spaces.

SITUATION

- A family of five needs more space.
- Huge amounts of produce from the family garden must be canned and preserved.
- Family and friends gather to join in the work simultaneously.

SOLUTIONS

- Create a sizable 23×18½-foot kitchen.
- Bring in a massive island for produce.
- Introduce multiple workstations built around two refrigerators and a pair of fridge drawers, three sinks, and a host of pullout cutting boards.

1

KITCHEN

After

1 *Book bindings cut from old cookbooks are glued onto black posterboard and fitted into some cabinet fronts, concealing a stash of less-sightly supplies behind them. A swing-arm faucet at the range makes filling big stockpots easy.*

2 *Pullout cutting boards close to the sinks and stovetop mean you never have to take up precious counter space for chopping.*

3 *A shallow pullout pantry puts odd-size spice containers within reach.*

4 *A butcher-block-top nesting cart on casters creates yet another workstation that you can roll to wherever you need it.*

5 *A section of marble countertop makes a handy baking cen-ter. The center also has an outlet for appliances, an upper-shelf microwave, and a pullout cutting board that's handy for resting cookie sheets as they're loaded with rolled dough cutouts.*

1

Designed for *Harmony*

TWO COOKS

Tripping over one another does not contribute to happy experiences in the kitchen. Whether a couple shares in the cooking or one leads and the other follows, both will have more fun if they can be together without threat of collisions. Separate cooking and cleanup/storage centers, plus an island that divides those spaces but is adjacent to both, helps two people with culinary creativity.

SITUATION

- A couple wants to work together in the kitchen without being in each other's way.
- One leads and cooks, while the other chops and cleans up.

SOLUTIONS

- Design a moderately sized kitchen.
- Incorporate a J-shape, two-sink island plan with work centers that don't overlap.

After

1 This J-shape plan provides plenty of counter space. The island multitasks as a work surface and dining space.

2 Electrical outlets rim the overhang on the island's top—making them handy yet out of sight.

3 A broad, deep drawer houses spice containers.

4 A slide-out shelf beneath the microwave makes a great landing spot for hot items and also doubles as a cutting board.

5 Divider grids protect a set of everyday china, stacked conveniently in a drawer, from sliding about.

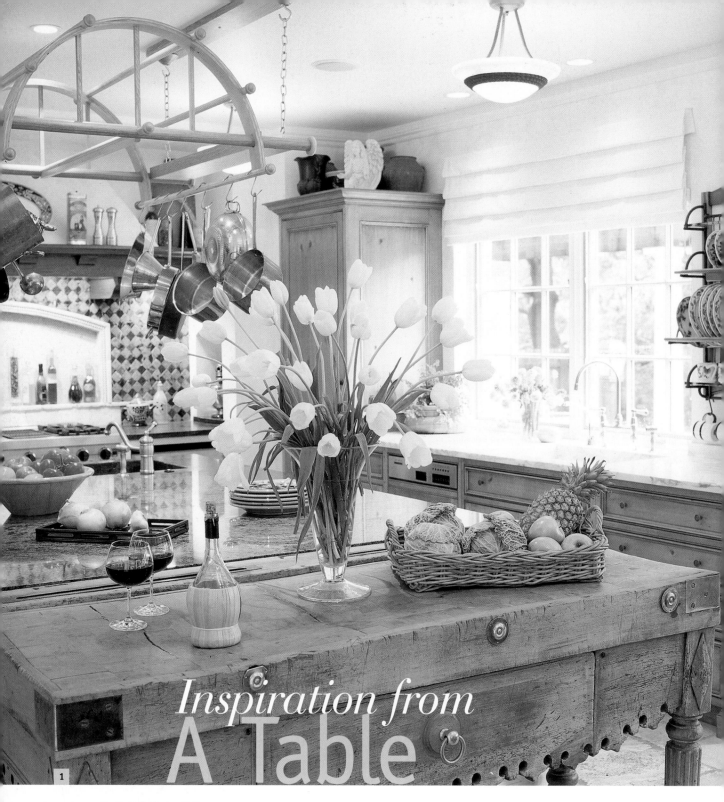

Inspiration from
A Table

1

DESIGNER

Without a client's hopes and dreams to respond to, internationally known kitchen designer Mick De Giulio found himself searching for a place to start creating a kitchen for his own family. Six months into pondering various looks and layouts, De Giulio, who believes that a kitchen's design should be very personal, happened onto a butcher's table. "We took one look at the table and said, 'This is our kitchen!' then built the design around it." If you, too, are overwhelmed with myriad choices, follow De Giulio's lead, choosing and using what you love.

SITUATION

- **The existing 12×12-foot kitchen is too small for the live-in area desired.**
- **Familiarity with many kitchen layouts and materials makes it hard for a designer to choose among them for his own home.**
- **With plenty of room for an addition of any kind, the designer has to find something to inspire the new space.**

1 This inspirational butcher's table becomes the end of an 8½×5½-foot center island. The kitchen incorporates seven different cabinet styles.

2 The hood's design is inspired by a pergola in the garden. Backsplash tiles are set close without grout. Recesses to both sides of the counter have electrical outlets. Open-style range-side drawers keep contents within view. The floor is made up of 18-inch squares of tumbled stone in a running bond pattern.

3 The former kitchen is now a pantry. Sky-blue painted cupboard backs suggest a sunny day, while the sandblasted-glass fronts only hint at what's contained within.

4 A gas fireplace adds to the allure of the space. Both a dining area and cushy chairs make room for family activities.

SOLUTIONS

- Turn the former kitchen into a pantry.
- Add on a kitchen/family room.
- Look for inspiration everywhere. For the De Giulios, inspiration came in the form of an old butcher's table. For others, it might come in a light fixture, book cover, landscape photo, or even a product package.
- Mix surfaces and cabinet styles for variety.

Multipurpose
Family Kitchen

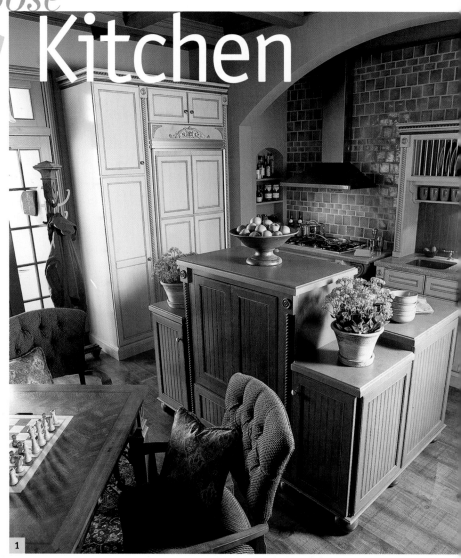

OPEN

Compartmentalized, single-function rooms might be fun if you're a kid building a shoebox home for dolls, but they're not if you're a family who likes to spend time together. Once this space was opened up for a kitchen/family room, a smart layout and Arts and Crafts-style elements were used to create an inviting, attractive, and functional space.

SITUATION

- The existing kitchen is roomy but is broken up and compartmentalized.
- There is no space for the family to gather and relax together.
- The kitchen's style is dingy and utilitarian.

SOLUTIONS

- Knock down walls separating the breakfast and laundry areas.
- Rework the larger, square room as a kitchen open to a sitting room and home office.
- Incorporate elegant style features throughout the opened-up space to boost appeal.

Before

KITCHEN
BREAKFAST
LAUNDRY

After

OFFICE
SITTING
TV
PANTRY
FOOD PREP

1 Creamy white cabinet fronts conceal the refrigerator and contribute to the room's mix of surfaces and unfitted style. Dish storage over the sink makes cleanup a cinch.

2 Furniturelike supports and an extended work surface bolster the built-in oven and cooktop.

3 The comfy library style of this family area is ideal for doing homework, reading the paper, or visiting with the cook.

4 A new pantry is steps closer to the kitchen. Island doors facing the table conceal a TV and VCR. A gentle arch motif is repeated over the doors, range, and hearth.

5 A home office tucks into an open alcove in front of the fireplace.

Confections & Company

1

PARTY

Nationally known pastry chef and cookbook author Emily Luchetti isn't one of those "get-out-of-my-kitchen-while-I-create" chefs.

In fact, her new kitchen encourages interaction with guests during meal preparation. Gutting most of the house and starting over created room for this hardworking enclave. The new kitchen features clean lines, a pleasing mix of warm wood cabinets and countertops, and sleek commercial appliances.

- The homeowner is a professional pastry chef who loves to create recipes and entertain small and large groups while she cooks; ample space is needed.
- The kitchen lacks adequate counter, refrigerator, and storage space.
- There's no connection between the kitchen and other public spaces in the house.

S O L U T I O N S

- Install a pair of islands to create distinct food preparation, dining, and snack/beverage areas.
- Install a marble-top baking counter and a pair of generous-size ovens.
- Create a separate cleanup space.
- Drop the wall between the living room and adjoining dining room.
- Visually separate the kitchen and living room with architectural elements.

1 Clean-line maple cabinetry is stained two colors, gray and yellow, for variety. The countertops feature a mix of surfaces—mahogany, marble, stainless steel—depending on their function. Big wall ovens and commercial-size refrigeration meet the needs of a pro chef. A rack-and-hook system keeps utensils easily visible and within reach. The kitchen's main island offers both food preparation and dining space.

2 Marble countertops for rolling dough define the baking center.

3 A cutting board and three-tiered sink are convenient for fruit and vegetable preparation.

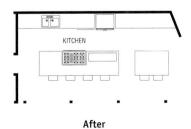

KITCHEN

After

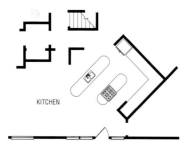

KITCHEN

Before

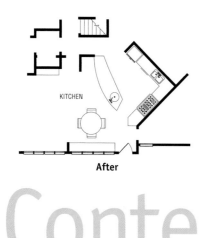

KITCHEN

After

Cook's
Contemporary

PARTY

Created by a serious cook who wanted to entertain in Euro-contemporary style, this kitchen features sleek architect-designed lines, abstract shapes, and ample work and storage space. It makes a strong individual statement and was easy to achieve within the existing lines of the generic condo kitchen it replaced.

1

SITUATION

- A gourmet cook wants an individualistic, upscale space to share her culinary creations with friends.
- There's a large collection of glassware and dishes to be displayed.
- Double islands block traffic in the kitchen.
- Appliances and storage space are not adequate for the cook's needs.

SOLUTIONS

- Custom-made European cabinets define a sleek, upscale look.
- Install lighted cabinets with frosted-glass fronts and glass shelves to store and display dishes and glassware.
- Replace the double islands with one island large enough to cook on and serve from; its curved shape keeps it from appearing too massive.
- Install a 48-inch commercial range and refrigerator plus two fridge doors in the island to handle food storage and prep.

2

1 *European beech cabinets have full-length stainless handles for easy opening. Stainless steel clads the appliances, range hood, and island. Low-voltage halogen lights arc over the cabinets.*
2 *A TV and toaster hide behind a tambour door when not in use.*
3 *Frosted-glass cabinet fronts make dishes a subtle part of the kitchen scene—and make selecting dishes easy. Clerestory windows echo the cabinets' glass grid pattern.*
4 *The granite-top island is nearly 4 feet at its widest point, offering enough room to set up a buffet and still have space to cook. A deep vegetable sink combined with two refrigerated drawers makes preparing fresh greens quick and easy.*

29

1

Island in
Pantry Out

LIVE-IN

Sometimes what you have is close to what you need—but not close enough. That was the case with this kitchen, which formerly had an island, a pantry, and a second sink. Even so, it didn't work: The cook's back was to guests when she cooked, there was never enough space to work, and the decor was unattractive. A fresh layout and new cabinets, surfaces, and lighting changed all that. Now a just-right party kitchen resides inside the same four walls.

SITUATION

- Guests are frequent in the kitchen, but sufficient space for them does not exist.
- The small angular island isn't practical.
- The large pantry is poorly designed; the shelves aren't large enough to hold large items, such as a platter.
- The desk on the pantry wall impedes the walkway between the dining and family rooms.
- The laminate cabinets are dated and worn.

SOLUTIONS

- Swap the existing island for a larger bilevel island that has a cooktop, work surfaces, and a snack counter.
- Replace the pantry wall with a handsome hutch and storage area.
- Fit the kitchen with a blend of stained and painted cabinetry and contemporary decorative touches.

2

3

1 The bilevel island lets the cook visit with guests, yet keeps visitors from stepping into the work area. The island cooktop allows for more counter space.

2 A blend of lighting elements— pendants, recessed cans, and undercabinet fixtures—provides mood control. The kitchen glows at night, which is a nice touch for parties.

3 Rust-color concrete countertops combine with cherry cabinets and iridescent backsplash tiles to create a warm glow. Tucked in at an angle, the desk doesn't get in the way.

Asian
Influence

1 Black composite-frame windows trimmed in maple offer views of the garden, bringing the outdoors inside. Three skylights shower the eating area with gentle, natural light.
2 Shoji-look panels in the cabinet doors above the sink and hutch-style cabinets in the butler's pantry help carry the Asian theme. White oak floors and pale maple cabinets appear neutral and clean. Black fixtures maintain consistency of hues.
3 Black bullnose trim on cupboards creates a strong horizontal line, stopping just short of the ceiling. Shoji-look panels are fitted with fiberglass inserts that resemble rice paper. Lighted from within, the panels cast a soft glow.

STYLE FIRST

The desire for a particular aesthetic and ambience led to the remodeling of this kitchen and its adjacent rooms. Its owners, two busy people who sought calm and reinvigoration from their home, wanted a kitchen area that reflected their interest in Asian style and ideals. To achieve that goal, kitchen designers rearranged the home's first floor and used a design motif—pale flooring and cabinets, black accents, paper-backed shoji panels and grids—that furthers the style's Asian influence.

Continued on page 34

1

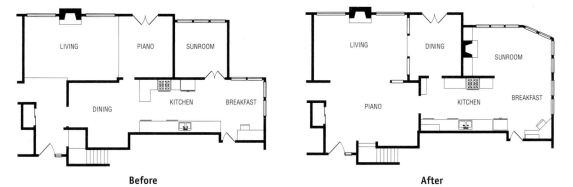

Before

After

If your kitchen feels a bit worn and dreary,

but it has enough space for your needs and a good layout, you may be able to update its look for a lot

See page 42

less trouble and expense than you assume. The kitchens featured in this section prove that some relatively quick and easy changes can have major impact. In one instance, you'll see how you can easily install glass fronts and interior lighting in many types of existing cabinets to visually expand your space as well as turn your glassware into a sparkling display. In another, a single well-placed skylight transforms a murky galley kitchen from dowdy to dramatic. Yet another study shows how recycled and reused materials work well to create authentic and vintage ambience. You'll also see the benefits of kitchens remade with an eye for attitude as much as efficiency. Packed with

See page 52

real-life applications of clever ideas, this chapter will help you shake up your kitchen with vibrance and vitality.

Refresh

1

This formerly utilitarian 1940s kitchen gets a big boost from some relatively minor changes. An arched tiled niche over the range creates visual impact reminiscent of '40s architecture, and a broom closet is sacrificed to make room for the refrigerator, formerly located too far outside kitchen confines.

The most dramatic moves in this kitchen are its soft furnishings and the color scheme. Chocolate, caramel, and cream make a sophisticated, neutral combination that is fresh and clean. Chocolate functions in the same way black does, creating a clean silhouette, but with brown's warmth and nuance. Though the sole pattern in this kitchen is folksy gingham, the overall ambience is one of tailored sophistication. Just the right amount of detailing keeps things interesting: ribbon edging at the blind's edge, a stripe across banquette curtains, and linen apron skirts beneath the sink and island. Piping on the ivory banquette and ottoman upholstery underscores the controlled, soft look. This chocolate and caramel color scheme makes for a space that's sophisticated—and as luscious as a turtle sundae.

1 The arched niche over the range includes an inset to hold spices and oils. The mahogany-top island gets a functional boost from a bowl-style sink and gooseneck faucet. Underneath, a gently gathered skirt of linen conceals shelves of pots, pans, and bakeware.

2 A U-shape banquette with two ottomans seats more diners in this small space than a table and chairs would. At the window, ivory curtains accented with a gingham and chocolate ribbon stripe flank a gingham blind. A goldfish bowl hangs from the banquette's lighting fixture—pure fun! The floor covering beneath the table is a piece of pale green, wipe-clean linoleum with a yarn fringe.

3 This kitchen sports its original cabinets. Recessed panels were removed to make way for glass insets. Caramel-hue gingham lines the cabinet backs, nicely offsetting the ivory dishes.

4 Beneath a farmhouse-style sink and marble countertops, this arched storage space sports a fabric apron that's linen on one side, gingham on the other.

5 Walls behind the banquette are padded and covered with linen and ribbon, creating a tackboard for mementos. The ribbon grid echoes the table's criss-crossed base and the gingham's squares.

6 At the window, chocolate-color ribbon defines the scalloped edge of the caramel gingham roller blind.

Simmering
With Color

This tiny kitchen's location in a San Francisco multiunit building meant adding space was out of the question. As a result, its renewal called on light and color to transform the shadowy, closetlike space into a warm and inviting one. Now enlivened by hues of paprika, saffron, and sage, this pint-size kitchen bubbles over with textural interest and contemporary convenience.

The extra light and newly found function come from a single deft step: moving one of the kitchen's doorways from the side to the end of the room. The new 6-foot-wide doorway off the foyer opens the small kitchen, improves traffic flow, and captures light from adjoining spaces. Walling up the old opening makes room for additional storage, a larger cooktop, and continuous countertops. It also allows the inclusion of a small breakfast table.

The room's colors are cued by rough-hewn slate tiles used for both the floor and the backsplash. Toned-down variations of the slate's green, gold, and rust veining echo across the budget-friendly flat maple cabinetry and laminate countertops. Cherry, butterscotch, and green aniline dyes add a custom color-wash finish to the cabinets and allow the natural wood grain to show through. (For more information on aniline dyes, see page 89.)

A Glass *Act*

When purchasing new cabinets, one budget-wise way to get a custom look for minimal cost is to specify glass fronts for some or all of the doors. Or, if you're refinishing existing cabinets, you may be able to have a local cabinetmaker cut out door panels and replace them with glass relatively inexpensively. Either way, adding glass to cabinetry lets you vary texture and gives your kitchen a greater sense of depth. Depending on whether you choose transparent or translucent glass, you can show off dishes or collectibles (transparent) or merely hint at their colors and shapes (frosted or patterned translucent). Adding accent lighting behind either type of glass takes the look one step further.

Before

KITCHEN

After

KITCHEN

1 *Richly variegated slate tiles set the color palette for this warm, contemporary kitchen. Using the same tiles for both the floor and the backsplash gives the kitchen's scheme a pleasing continuity.*

2 *The 12×12 slate tiles range in thickness from $^3/_8$ to $^5/_8$ inches. A rustic counterpart to sleek stainless-steel surfaces, they are sealed to prevent staining. The cooktop is shallow enough to allow for a storage drawer to be mounted directly below the counter.*

3 *Reeded-glass panels, inset into cabinet doors near the sink area, provide relief from runs of solid cabinets. Aniline dye on the plain maple cabinet fronts and two colors of laminate on the countertops give these budget-friendly materials custom appeal.*

4 *Tearing out a lower bank of cabinets and moving the refrigerator across the room made it possible to carve out a new doorway and create a small corner eating area with a bistro table that's bolted to the floor.*

A Flood of
Ideas

When the water pipes burst and saturated the 1,200-square-foot interior of this house, its interior required complete rework and repair. The kitchen receives a great new look for surprisingly little cost by using inexpensive metals in innovative ways—providing the gleam of stainless for a lot less gold.

The result is a hip, metal-accented kitchen, with a down-home twist: The shiny, stamped-metal sheeting used for the backsplash and wainscoting is embossed with a brick pattern reminiscent of tin ceilings in old buildings. Sold as inexpensive skirting material for manufactured homes, the amount required for the whole kitchen cost only $75.

A stainless-front range replaced a flood-damaged white model, but the white refrigerator survived, so it was wrapped in galvanized steel—much less costly than buying a new stainless appliance. That transformation suggested the use of galvanized panels in the new custom cabinets. The material's variegated, almost crystalline sparkle complements the texture of the stamped wainscoting, and now the whole room glistens and gleams.

Galvanized into Action Metal is in vogue these days, and galvanized sheet steel—a country cousin to stainless—has an informal charm all its own. It has been used for eons in a variety of hardworking residential, farm, and commercial applications that range from watering cans to ductwork and corrugated roofs. The material is rust-resistant, readily available, relatively inexpensive, and easy to work with. Any sheet metal fabricator can wrap a refrigerator in the metal, for instance. The trick is in taking precise measurements, so have your fabricator measure your project.

For metal-accented cabinetry, order the cabinetry minus the recessed panels (or remove the recessed panels from existing cabinetry) as if you are going to put glass in them. Then have a fabricator measure and cut panels to size. Install the panels by running a bead of caulk around the back perimeter of the panel to secure.

1 A stainless-steel restaurant prep table looks great and performs well as a freestanding island. A wine box on casters beneath the island serves as a rolling "drawer" that's accessible from all four sides. Black and white tiles lend a crisp geometry to the room and complement the playful, chalkboard-front dishwasher. The countertops are poured concrete. The contractor used aluminum angle iron as the form, then left the angle in place to form a bright, decorative edge.

2 Robust red on the walls and wooden furniture balance the use of metals and keep the space from appearing cold.

3 An old linen press lends warmth and charm to this corner; old metal canisters, pans, and silver wire bins tie it in with the metal wainscoting.

Function & Fashion

Function drove the remodel of this formerly dingy, dated kitchen in a 1925 house. Professional-grade stainless-steel appliances were a priority for the homeowner, as were granite countertops for frequent baking sessions. The granite continues up the wall a few inches, providing a short backsplash that gives way to a painted wall. The kitchen's original white cabinets were tossed in favor of the warmth of straightforward, recessed panel maple cabinetry fitted with simple brushed steel knobs and bin pulls.

The cabinet's crown molding is a nod to traditional styling found elsewhere in the house. On the floor, a honey-hue, straight-planked hardwood floor brings in more warmth. Recessed can lights and undercabinet lighting strips are nearly invisible save one frosted white pendant over the table. Food, kitchenware, and small appliances are the sole accents in this well-organized space that is wonderfully simple.

1 One corner comprises the kitchen's new cooking center, smartly situated next to the cleanup center. Open vertical storage dividers echo the strong lines of the cabinetry. Both are graced with crown molding. Surfaces appear simple and clutter free: no nonsense, no frills.
2 The reworked kitchen packs loads of efficiency into a slightly stretched footprint. Pushing a wall into an adjacent bathroom makes room for the big stainless refrigerator.
3 Building a table into the small wall provides a place for casual meals and doing homework. The surface also functions as a work island.
4 Kitchen tools—pots and pans hung on a rack—also serve as ornaments over the sink. Cleaning up after cooking is simple: Dirty cookware goes from the stove to the sink or dishwasher, then back to the rack.
5 Here's a smart move: A bold, clean-lined, removable slat panel conceals a radiator beneath the table. Above it, a small ledge supports a tiny TV and VCR.

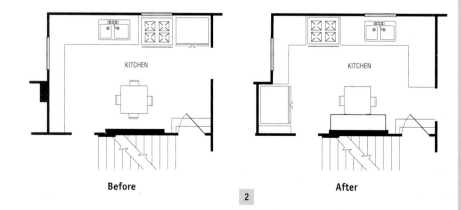

Before

After

2

3
4
5

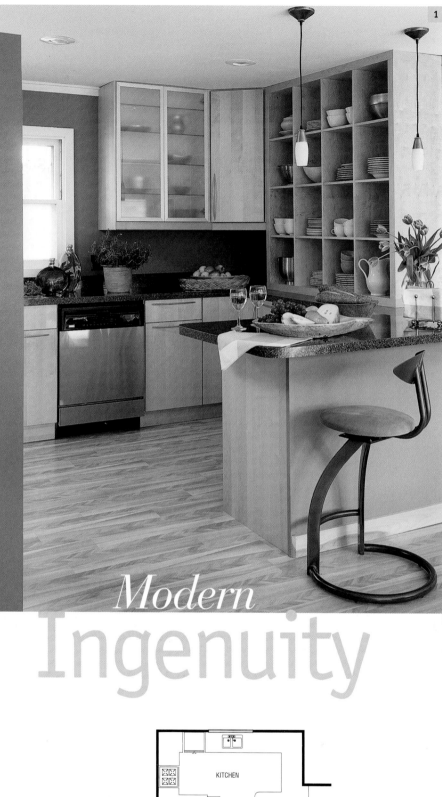

A European bistro look was the goal for this now spiffy kitchen created within a 1950s ranch house. The look did not require a fat wallet: Birch Swedish-modern cabinets came from a home furnishings retailer, were delivered by mail, and installed by the homeowners. Gloss laminate counters in faux granite look luxe without the expense. That cubby wall? It's actually a bookshelf, purchased and installed after discovering that more storage space was needed. The flooring is a dressy patterned hardwood laminate that extends into the living room. The red wall that separates a work counter from the living area is a gutsy touch that gives the kitchen a visual kick. If you need rationale to make such a bold color move, choose a hue from a nearby fabric or artwork.

Modern
Ingenuity

KITCHEN

3

4

5

1 The kitchen opens into the living room; the peninsula/breakfast bar also is used as a cocktail bar for parties. The red wall conceals the kitchen's main food prep counter. Frosted-glass fronts on some cabinets hint at contents without totally revealing them. Over the sink, the lower half of the double-hung windows is frosted,eliminating the need for window treatments.

2 A modern-style, one-piece faucet serves the stainless-steel sink and its built-in colander.

3 A C-shape kitchen plan, open at one end, creates an efficient work space for homeowners who like to entertain frequently.

4 A fresh take on open shelves, the grid of cubbies is ideal for dishware, cookbooks, pantry items, and displaying collections.

5 Kitchen tools are handy without cluttering the counter, thanks to a backsplash rail system. The granite-look countertops and backsplash are actually glossy finished laminate.

Galley Ho!

Though there's nothing inherently wrong with the long and narrow galley kitchen, it is the most oft-lamented of kitchen layouts. In fact, there's a lot that's right when it comes to the layout. It's compact and efficient, with everything you need close at hand, and longer versions usually offer the option of a cozy eating nook at an end. The configuration works well in countless floor plans—including scads of ranch homes, such as this 1950s San Francisco example.

The problem is not so much how galley kitchens work, but how they often feel: gloomy and dead-ended, especially those fitted with dark cabinetry and too few windows. Here's a project that proves you don't have to do too much to turn your blind alley of a kitchen into a light-filled space.

A large skylight and new cabinets with a finish of whitewashed, distressed alder take much of the credit for transforming this kitchen's character from gloomy to light. The soft-washed finish has more visual texture than solid white paint and is more forgiving because nicks and scrapes simply blend in. A quarter-sawn oak floor replaces boring beige linoleum. Finally, counters were topped with concrete tiles in an earthy terra-cotta color.

Along with changes in surfaces, the eating nook adopted a centered window for a lighter aspect and view of the garden, along with a built-in bookcase and banquette. The other end of the room gained a built-in refrigerator and a hutch. In between, two rectangular columns that divide the kitchen from the adjacent dining room double as cabinets and provide storage and architectural interest.

1

Before

After

2

3

Concrete Tiles Are an *Option*

The use of concrete for countertops is a burgeoning trend: The material is natural, durable, and incredibly stable. In addition, it can be custom-mixed, almost like paint, in just about any color you desire. But the weight, complexity, and mess involved in installing cast-in-place slab countertops can be daunting.

If you're one of the daunted, consider concrete tiles instead. They install just like regular tile, but retain much of the heft and durability of a slab. Plus, the patterns and grout lines offer a pleasing, traditional detail that slab installations lack. (You can seal both the tiles and the grout against stains.) A final benefit: Because you buy and lay out the tiles already cast, cured, and stained, you know exactly what the finished countertop will look like before you begin.

1 *Aside from the breakfast nook's window, the only object to be relocated was the refrigerator, keeping project costs low.*

2 *Because it was too small for a standard table and chairs, the eating nook features a banquette. Built-in display space for cookbooks and accessories adds a warm, personal touch.*

3 *The wall between the kitchen and the adjacent dining room had already been removed during a previous remodel; a breakfast bar took its place. Taking a good move one step further, columns of cabinetry were added to each end of the bar, increasing visual interest and storage space.*

Fresh Twists

When your kitchen needs a lift but major remodeling is out of the question, wake up the space with inexpensive surface treatments, such as paint and fabric. The results promise to be more vibrant and satisfying than you might have imagined—for little financial investment.

Paint. You can paint almost every surface—not just metal or wood cabinets, but wall paneling, wood floors, and even countertops and appliances—if you use special, highly durable epoxy finishes. Visit a quality paint supplier to see the products available for your special needs. If you'd rather not do the job yourself, seek out companies that specialize in refinishing cabinets and countertops and ask for an estimate for the job.

Fabric. Textiles bring softness and texture into the kitchen by way of curtains, tablecloths, chair cushions, and window toppers. To keep your kitchen's look fresh even longer, you can make different sets to suit the seasons. If you enjoy more unconventional fabric applications, pull off one or more lower cabinet doors and replace them with a shirred fabric skirt; hang the skirt from a rod mounted at the top or use hook-and-loop tape. Or replace glass cabinet fronts with shirred fabric.

Lighting. Undercabinet lighting is not just for high-tech, freshly installed kitchens. It's easy to mount either fluorescent or halogen fixtures beneath existing cabinets. Fluorescent light is diffuse and it minimizes shadows; halogen fixtures create a bright white light that's perfect for task lighting, yet dimmable for mood lighting. Visit a home center to find individual lights or lighting strips to suit your needs.

Hardware. Polish, paint, or replace your cabinet hardware, thinking of it as jewelry for your kitchen. Choices are available in all styles and price ranges, from both local home improvement centers and catalog and online retailers. If your fresh hardware choice is particularly eye-catching, consider using it sparingly for emphasis—for instance just on sink-side upper cabinets—supporting it with a simpler choice elsewhere in the kitchen.

Color *Combo*

Want to find a sassy color theme for your kitchen? Design books and magazines are great resources, but you'll find even more ideas if you study commonplace items. Hunt color themes in these predesigned sources:

- Bedding and bath displays
- Children's books
- Clothing displays
- Event posters
- Fabric stores and collections
- Food and product packages
- Housewares department
- Pottery, paintings
- Team uniforms

If you plan to make fabric part of your decor, include a trip to the fabric store and look for yardage in the color schemes you like. Then, if you decide to paint, take your swatches and other sources of inspiration to a paint supplier to identify just the right color to complete your scheme.

Cabinet painting ideas:
- Color on white
- Two hues of the same color
- Contrasting colors, such as yellow and blue, or red and green
- Analogous colors that rub shoulders on the color wheel, such as orange and red, yellow and orange, or green and blue
- Solid cabinet walls behind doors in a palette of colors
- Solid cabinet walls behind doors painted with stripes, checks, or dots

Cupboard back ideas:
- Use a stencil to apply a motif.
- Apply paint in a soft color. In the same way pale sky blue sets off a ceiling, it adds subtle light and mood to a cupboard back. Consider soft yellow or pink, or whatever color complements your scheme.
- Tack up some fabric. If you're using fabric in your kitchen, choose a coordinate and use clear thumbtacks to affix a flat stretch of fabric on the surface of the cabinet back.

2

3

1 *A bright blue and white color scheme creates a farmhouse-fresh ambience in this roomy kitchen. Cut-to-fit beaded-board panels, adhered to the backsplash with a liquid adhesive, add even more farm-style charm. A paper border plus a mix of fabric coordinates adds much-needed, small-scale pattern to cabinets and the self-stick vinyl tile floor. Letters for the decorative words above the cupboards were made with the help of a computer and copier, then filled in with colored marking pens.*

2 *Give the backs of your glass-fronted display cabinets some TLC and you'll add interesting detail and dimensional depth to your kitchen. In this cupboard, the solution is as simple as contact paper. Its abstract, graphic motif is a subtle nod to the room's black-and-white scheme, and it complements the colorful dishes.*

3 *A faux wood laminate countertop hardly gets noticed in the face of this citrusy kitchen scheme, inspired by the vibrant paintings that hang over the window. Apple green and soft sunny yellow accentuate the scalloped cabinet panels and trim pieces, the beaded-board walls, and display shelves; white trim ties the space to the rest of the house and keeps the look crisp. Over the windows, yards of yellow fabric are knotted, twisted, and swagged to soften the windows. Hot shots of pink, prominent in the paintings, pop up on the hand-painted floorcloth.*

1

Blending Old
With New

2

Proving that almost no house is too far gone for renovation, this kitchen in an 800-year-old house in the village of Mougins, France, emerged from a building so dilapidated it shook with every footstep. Although the house required a complete gutting and massive structural work to ensure its safety and survival, the goal was to re-create a rustic look while providing 21st-century function.

Even if your kitchen only looks and feels 800 years old, this kitchen offers some good examples of how to blend old interior surfaces into modernized space. It also provides a glimpse of the French Provençal style.

Some of the charm evident in this room originates from the house: True to its initial footprint, the kitchen is narrower at one end than the other. The rest, however, is credited to careful craftsmanship. The builders replaced wood beams with concrete, for example, but they saved beams to be put on display as ceiling beams, door lintels, and a mantel-like lip on the range hood. Carpenters rebuilt the walls and ceilings flat and true, but replastered unevenly to mimic the wavering structure of a centuries-old building. At ground level, the floor is finished in antique hexagonal tiles known as *tomettes*, which are characteristic of period homes in that part of France.

Don't Throw That Out! Before they may legally practice medicine, physicians take the Hippocratic oath: First, do no harm. Those who venture to renovate an old house would do well to take a similar oath: Throw nothing away—at least not until the project is complete. Even if a crumbling bit of ornament or structure can no longer serve its original purpose, it might provide an invaluable clue to the building's age, style, materials, construction, or builder. Moreover, such detritus may end up serving a new purpose in the finished project.

In this case, the owners proved wise to save the home's original beams. No longer strong enough to safely support the building, the beams live on as decorative elements that tell the story of the 800-year-old craftsmanship and 800 hundred years of weathering that makes the house what it is. Furthermore, unique finds like these cost nothing and, because they were on site when renovation started, their particular shapes and features—the gentle bow in the beam used as the door lintel *right*, for example, or the huge knot that's centered over the range—could be incorporated in the design from the start.

Before you gut a historic structure, make a place for sifting and saving what you take out. Share the contents of your storeroom with your architect, designer, and contractor, encouraging them to use what they see to match the materials, design, and construction techniques of their new work to that of the old. Also encourage them to reuse old materials—such as molding and first-growth lumber—whenever possible.

1 *All-wood custom cabinets match a beloved antique cabinet in the adjoining dining room. Antique* tomette *floor tiles recall the earth tones of the landscape and the sunny glow that settles on the French countryside as afternoon turns to evening.*

2 *Screen and rooster silhouettes add Provençal detailing to the cabinets, as does their distressed paint finish.*

3 *Sunny, hand-glazed and painted ceramic tile and rough-plastered, painted walls add to this kitchen's old-world charm. Lava stone countertops are painted Provençal yellow-gold. Metal pulls and knobs in classic French shapes increase the textural mix.*

4 *The rough-hewn door lintel was once one of the home's original beams.*

53

On the
Walls

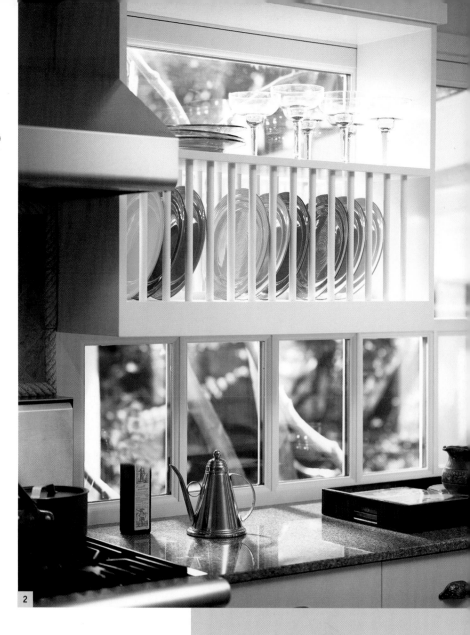

Who says walls and cabinets can't convey sunlight? They do in this kitchen, where cabinets with glass fronts and backs hang over window walls to pull in any light the Northwest region has to offer. The window walls, plus new cabinets, surfaces, and built-ins, dramatically change the disposition of this kitchen without needing to alter its footprint a bit. The addition of a freestanding island boosts the kitchen's efficiency, making it workable for all three cooks who use it. Hung on the dining wall, a huge French poster fulfills the job of focal point, anchoring a mass of built-in shelving that keeps books, pottery, and other collectibles in full view.

Continued on page 56

2

Before   **After**

1

1 *The new freestanding island adds food prep space and makes for a tighter, more efficient work core. Two expansive window walls on either side of the range replace two small windows along the working side of the kitchen.*

2 *To clean the window behind this plate rack, dowels slide out of the fixed top shelf, and the lower front panel is removable.*

3 *New built-ins stretch across the formerly blank dining wall to set the scene for attractive storage and display space; they also position the kitchen table for patio and garden views. Dark-stained oak floors and a floral rug with a black background are rich counterpoints to the creamy white cabinets and colorful pottery. The overall look of this kitchen is cheerful and bright, yet in no way shrill.*

1 A freestanding island, stained green and styled with turned legs and an apron detail, makes it easy to move food from refrigerator to counter to sink or stove. Glass-fronted and -backed cabinets hover over thermal pane windows, taking advantage of any available light. Notice the limestone backsplash over the range: The 4×4 tiles remain unsealed to reveal more of their texture.

2 Three styles of pewter-finish hardware—bin pulls on the drawers, apple-shape knobs on the island, and twisted pulls on the refrigerator doors—enliven this kitchen.

3 Can lights, a simple yet elegant chandelier, and French doors take care of lighting day and night. The grand scale of the early 1900s poster makes a commanding focal point in the kitchen.

Outlets Away Here's an ingenious, three-part alternative to peppering your walls with somewhat unsightly electrical outlets. This kitchen features only one wall outlet, and it's hidden inside the appliance garage. But a continuous outlet strip hidden under the upper cabinets provides plug-ins every 4 feet, and you couldn't ask for more places to plug in. A single outlet in the floor serves the freestanding island, *above left*.

57

Season
With Color

Located on California's Coronado Island, a dowdy ceramic-and-linoleum galley kitchen, dated 1954, lacked the cottage-by-the-sea look it deserved. An affordable redo comprised of paint, fabric, accessories, and artwork seasoned the small space with vibrant color and breezy style.

1 *The banquette tabletop was embellished with ceramic tile and dish fragments for a colorful, custom accent.*

2 *Extra-deep countertops offer additional work and storage space yet required no expensive modifications to achieve: The cabinets were simply moved out from the wall to accommodate the large granite slab. Local artists lent their creative talents to this now-lively kitchen: One hand-painted the floorcloth, another fashioned the one-of-a-kind metal cabinet pulls.*

The makeover begins with the addition of vintage-style background elements, such as recycled maple flooring and white crown molding. Replacing a steel entry door with a white French door brings charm and light into the space, visually extending the kitchen's horizons to an adjoining courtyard. The cabinets sport new coats of bright white paint and new knobs, and they're pulled out 3 inches from the wall to create more counter space. A ¾-inch slab of granite tops them off. A pantry cabinet was relocated to an opposite wall to make room for a built-in banquette. To complete the restyling, a local artist spiced the space with a hand-painted floorcloth. A mosaic-tile table accents the banquette, and bright collectibles fill the shelves.

Easy Decorating

Breathe fresh personality into a tired kitchen scheme with these surface moves.

1. Add cushions, pillows, tablecloths, and napkins to underscore your color scheme. Soft furnishings and other fabric touches are an inexpensive way to brighten a space and bring in pattern.

2. Display favorite dishes, glassware, colorful cookbooks, and collectibles in glass-fronted cabinets and on windowsills and countertops. Open shelves are a great way to break up masses of cabinetry and display everything from colorful cookie jars to pottery.

3. Reserve wall space for artwork. Enliven a space with a Picasso print, or add color with family photographs. Illuminate what you display with lighting fixtures that complement the room's style, from casual galvanized metal pendants, such as the one shown *right,* to formal solid-brass chandeliers.

4. Spice up cabinetry with decorative knobs and pulls; they're like jewelry for your kitchen. The hardware featured in the kitchen *right* was custom-made, but you can find many options at home centers and through mail-order sources. Or, paint wooden knobs and pulls to match the decor.

It's All in the Attitude

The floor plan changed very little, but thanks to bold surface choices, dramatic curves, and sleek styling, this kitchen's attitude stepped into high gear.

The peninsula broke off from the wall to become a huge, multifunctional island, then stepped 2 feet into the spacious great-room. A small second island dropped in to bridge the gap between the working walls and the big island. The result is a kitchen that both looks grand and feels twice as big though all changes came about within existing walls.

Light maple cabinets and granite countertops are a naturally intriguing combination. The curved cabinets cost more than flat ones, but they give shape to a boxy room. A fourfold lighting plan allows for task and mood lighting: At the ceiling, a broadly flared skylight shaft spreads sunlight from the center of the room outward; recessed cans take over when the sun goes down; undercabinet lighting illuminates countertops; and a dramatic headband suspended from the ceiling directs halogen lighting onto the island.

KITCHEN

Before

KITCHEN

After

1 Once a worn, dark kitchen tucked into the corner of a large room, this remodeled space now attracts attention with its bold look, never failing to deliver efficiency as well. To the right of the double ovens, a warming drawer keeps meals hot beneath a marble baking counter, which is set at a low height.

2 No counter surface is more than a step away from another, thanks to the two-island plan. The small island is ideal for unloading groceries, and it stores plenty of food storage containers.

3 Juperno granite, on the countertops and backsplash, is dramatically striated. Though it inherently resists burns, scratches, and stains, it's also sealed for protection. A gooseneck cold-water faucet at the range eliminates the need to carry heavy pots of water from sink to stove.

4 Recycling is easy with a double-bin pullout.

5 Above the oven, vertical storage eliminates a pile-up of trays and shallow baking pans.

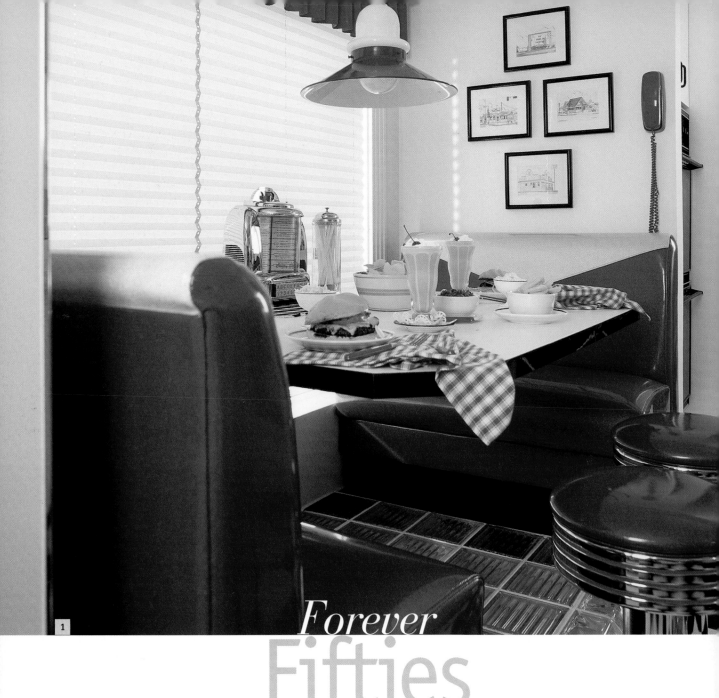

Forever
Fifties

A retro redo takes this 1957 St. Louis kitchen back to its midcentury roots with lots of checkerboard, chrome, lipstick red, and even some glowing neon. The result is a room that's just plain fun to be in. Made mostly with existing or inexpensive materials and ingenuity, this project generates a whole lot of wow for the dollar.

Old birch cabinets were treated to new laminate fronts with black plastic pulls. Carpenters reworked the lower cabinets to accommodate a microwave, retaining the position of the vintage cooktop. The tile backsplash, formerly all white, becomes a checkerboard when every other tile is cut out with a diamond saw, the backing replastered, and new black tiles are set in place. The complementary white checkerboard border above is cut from two rolls of a wallpaper pattern.

The eating area gets a big shot of red thanks to recycled cafeteria seats and new chrome stools reupholstered in matching red vinyl. Glass block replaces the flooring beneath the resulting booth, and fluorescent tubes that have been painted red shine through, bathing the whole eating area in a crimson glow. A custom-made neon fixture that blinks to life above the sink is the appropriate final touch.

1 What's a '50s diner without a booth and some counter stools? The upholstery on the benches matches that of the homeowner's '56 automobile. A glowing glass-block floor adds to the ambience.
2 The authentic inspiration for this '50s treatment was the 1957 cooktop. It's original to the house—and still in perfect working order.
3 A real conversation-starter, the red neon sign above the sink was custom-made. Beneath it, a glass-fronted cabinet shows off a collection of '50s dishes and glassware.

From Dated to Retro

Sometimes the most winning renovations are those that take what you already have and dress it to the nines. This kitchen was originally built in 1957, so the layout, scale, and cabinetry design already existed—as did a vintage cooktop outfitted with more little white buttons than a whole box of Chiclets. Plenty of people would completely redo such a "dated" kitchen and its Sputnik-era appliance too, but this project took the opposite approach, piling on '50s clichés and icons to a flamboyant, theatrical degree.

Do you have one of these dated kitchens from the 1970s? What the heck: Go retro. Date it even more. Haunt flea markets and salvage yards for harvest gold appliances, first-generation digital clocks with little flippy number wheels, orange lamps, shag carpeting, whatever you can find. Take the stuff back home and play around with it. When you feel the time warp suck you in, you know you're getting somewhere.

Whatever you do, though, don't be timid. Don't do it halfway. Be a purist. Be more '70s than the '70s. When it comes to retro, nothing succeeds like excess.

Looking Luxe for Less

A richly detailed kitchen needn't cost a life savings. Here's a study in how to use inexpensive, off-the-shelf supplies and components—such as molding, paint, wallpaper, and even bedposts—to transform a plain kitchen into a room that's rich with special touches.

This kitchen's wealth of detailing delights the eye and lends an old-world feel to a brand-new space. Granite countertops, custom cabinets, and high-quality fixtures make clear that this room wasn't built on a tight budget. Yet several of its most charming features, such as the island's carved legs, range hood detailing, and exquisite floor, are clever, low-cost extras that hold their own in expensive company.

1 Although the floor looks like slate, it's actually a faux stone ceramic tile, which is more durable, easier to care for, and less expensive than the real thing. Placing the tiles diagonally across the room adds to their visual interest. At the ceiling, sophisticated egg-and-dart molding caps the walls. White paint crisply defines the ceiling and the molding pattern accommodating the use of lower-cost, paint-grade millwork. A scrolled wallpaper border in a shade of brown and taupe graces the walls with an elaborate-yet-inexpensive touch of pattern.

2 The island's elaborately carved "legs" are actually discarded bedposts obtained at a furniture factory for $10 each. They contribute to the kitchen's unfitted, furniture-style look for less than the cost of stock cabinetry. The island features such traditional kitchen-island amenities as storage space and a warming drawer, but its tablelike design provides a more elegant look.

3 This custom range hood is a dramatic focal point, yet it was fabricated on-site from lumber, drywall, and stock millwork. Even the plaster medallion was an inexpensive, home-center purchase.

65

Give Your Kitchen a Fresh Dress

No matter how well your kitchen functions year after year, eventually you may want to give it a fresh dress. Changing your kitchen's surface treatments—walls, floors, cabinet fronts and finishes, countertops, fixtures, hardware, lighting, and furnishings—facilitates amazing transformations, reviving the room's look for years to come. A single kitchen samples two new looks on the following pages.

Getting Started

Before you begin any makeover project, preview your ideas on paper. It's easy and saves you lots of time, not to mention the agony of making expensive, incorrect choices. If you aren't an artist, don't fret; your drawings needn't be perfect.

• Photograph your kitchen as it exists now. Take just one shot of the kitchen that shows all the room's surface elements (or take a few, if needed).

• Enlarge the photo(s) to a size that fits on an 8½×11 sheet of paper. If you do not have access to a scanner or copier with this capability, go to a copy center.

• Lay a piece of tracing paper over your enlarged photograph, and use a sharp pencil to trace the kitchen's architectural features, along with any surfaces that will remain after your redo, onto the paper. For example, you would trace the outline of a checkerboard floor if you were certain that it was going to stay. Likewise, if you planned to replace light fixtures, you'd leave them out of the tracing.

• Photocopy the rendering several times to get numerous "blank canvases" on which to try out new looks.

• Use colored pencils to fill your kitchen surfaces with a fresh coat of paint in a new hue, a different kind of countertop material, or sparkling jewel-tone hardware.

• Sketch in any new light fixtures, furnishings, or window treatments you're considering.

• Support your previews by taping catalog clippings and material swatches alongside the sketch.

Continued on page 68

1 *A remodeling job completed years ago opened this kitchen to beautiful vistas of the park it overlooks. Runs of cabinetry, countertop, and appliances were reworked to free wall space for the windows and to boost the kitchen's functional efficiency. Today the floor plan still serves exceedingly well, but as for the kitchen's look, the high-contrast, terra-cotta plus green and white color scheme has simply been worn too long and has lost its appeal. A new look, just surface-deep, will refresh the kitchen for many more years to come. Take a look at the pages that follow to see how two new schemes infuse this weary kitchen with new personality.*

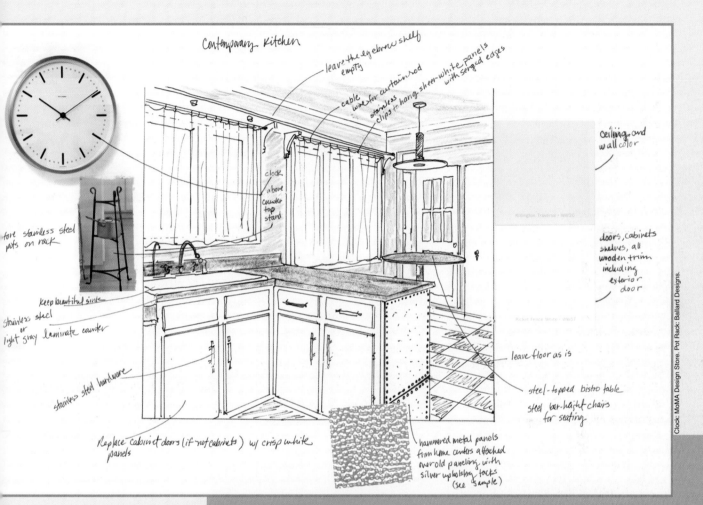

Contemporary Kitchen

leave the eyebrow shelf empty

cable wire for curtain rod

stainless clips to hang sheer white panels with serged edges

ceiling and wall color

Killington Traverse · WW20

clock above counter top stand

store stainless steel pots on rack

doors, cabinets shelves, all wooden trim including exterior door

keep beautiful sink

stainless steel or light gray laminate counter

Picket Fence White · WW57

leave floor as is

stainless steel hardware

steel-topped bistro table

steel bar-height chairs for seating

Replace cabinet doors (if not cabinets) w/ crisp white panels

hammered metal panels from home centers attached over old paneling with silver upholstery tacks (see sample)

Clock: MoMA Design Store. Pot Rack: Ballard Designs.

Contemporary Cues The first option explores an earthy, high color-and-contrast kitchen decked out for a contemporary look.

What Stays:
- Green and white checkerboard floor
- White cabinets
- White sink
- Silver gooseneck faucet
- Round halogen lamp over table

What Goes:
- Clutter on top of the eyebrow shelf
- Telephone
- Wooden trestle table
- Beaded-board cabinet backs (covered)
- Raised panel cabinet fronts
- Knobby cabinet hardware

What's New:
- Wall paint in soft, fresh mint green
- Sheer white curtains strung with stainless clips on cable wire
- Stainless clock between windows
- Stainless-steel bar-height table and chairs
- Hammered metal panels on cabinet backs attached with silver upholstery tacks
- Flat-fronted cabinet doors
- Sleek door and drawer pulls
- Light gray laminate countertop
- Stainless-steel pots and pans

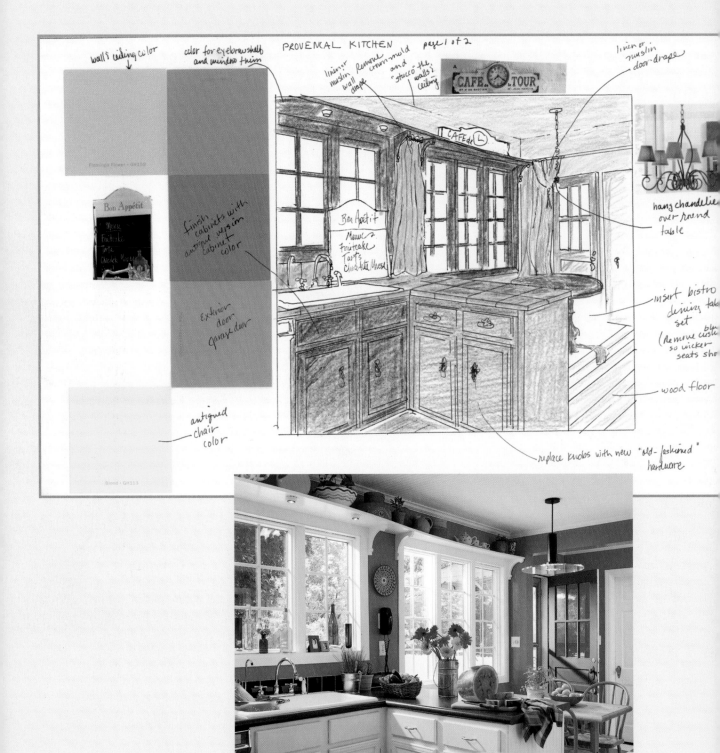

PROVENÇAL KITCHEN   page 1 of 2

walls ceiling color

color for eyebrow shelf and window trim

linen or muslin wall drape

Remove crown-mold and "stucco" the walls & ceiling

CAFE de TOUR

linen or muslin door-drape

hang chandelier over round table

finish cabinets with antiqued version cabinet color

Exterior door garage door

antiqued chair color

insert bistro dining table set (Remove cushion so wicker seats show

wood floor

replace knobs with new "old-fashioned" hardware

Provençal Plus

For an even more significant character change, here's the same kitchen dressed in soft, French countryside ambience.

What Stays:
- Cabinets
- White sink
- Silver gooseneck faucet

What Goes:
- Green and white checkerboard floor
- Round halogen lamp over table
- Green laminate countertops

What's New:
- Vibrant color scheme
- Blue-green antiqued finish on the cabinets
- Khaki paint on the window trim, eyebrow shelf, and interior doors
- Fresh medium green on the exterior door
- Apricot on the walls and ceiling
- Antiqued straw finish on the chairs
- Honey-color hardwood or faux wood floor
- Metal chandelier
- Linen or muslin drapes between windows and doors in apricot
- Old-fashioned hardware
- Cafelike accessories

PROVENCAL kitchen page 2 of 2

keep the table dark but make the chairs antique yellow shnon

put a tiered tray on the counter with a chambery breadboard, bread

prop eyebrow shelf with Rustic baskets if desired

Two-Tiered server: Crate&Barrell. All other products: Ballard Designs.

Perhaps your kitchen needs more than refreshing to achieve the look or function you want. Does the "work triangle" look more like a puzzle game? Are traffic patterns and appliance placement awkward or unworkable? Has your search for more room led to the stashing of small appliances, foodstuff, and dishes in the adjoining family room? In this chapter, you'll find one remodeling success after another, each presented with the guidance you need to get the results you're after. A remodel might mean that a wall has been knocked out to share light, borrow space, or simply improve the flow between an adjoining dining or family room. Or, it might mean adding a wall of windows to bring light and views into a formerly boxed-in space. A floor plan might need rearranging for efficiency. Whatever the case, these reworkings require a combination of moderate structural and cosmetic changes. The results are dramatic, so don't be shy: See what a little hammer swinging can accomplish!

See page 93

Remodel

Dysfunction
Junction

This kitchen in a charming 1950s ranch suffered severe functionality problems. The cramped layout was a U-shape, unfortunately hemmed in by a peninsula. Points where cabinetry intersected in three corners made for cavernous, hard-to-access storage space resulting in wasted space. In addition, there was no easy route from the kitchen to the adjacent dining room.

Topping off the issues, the only place to put the breakfast nook's table was right in front of the sliding door that led to a patio, rendering the door nonfunctional. Clearly the room was ripe for a remodeling.

A carefully thought-out and executed rearrangement of the existing space provided everything the owners wanted and more—without the cost of adding on. In addition to a spacious and efficient room, the kitchen gained a streamlined, contemporary look and now enjoys easy access to adjacent living spaces, lots of natural light, and great views.

Before   **After**

Steeling *the Show*

Previously if you sought stainless steel in the kitchen, you bought it in the form of a sink. Today, however, the material is used for everything from appliances and range hoods to countertops. This kitchen features metal cabinetry accents and a metal splatter board behind the cooktop. Here are a few options to consider if stainless catches your eye:

• A mirror finish has a bright, highly reflective appearance that stands out as an architectural detail, such as in this kitchen's cooktop splatter board. Scratches and fingerprints show up easily, though, so it's not a great choice for surfaces that receive a lot of wear.

• A brushed finish, either linear or random, is the standard choice for appliances and countertops; scratches and fingerprints are less likely to show.

• It's possible to apply translucent colors over the metal to suit your decor, but such finishes can also scratch like paint, can't be restored on-site, and reduce the steel's flexibility.

• Electroplating coats steel with other metals, such as copper or brass, but these coatings also reduce the metal's flexibility.

4

5

1 *The curved front of the island eeks out a few extra precious inches of preparation, serving, and dining space. For a streamlined look, a tambour door conceals a microwave oven next to the paneled refrigerator.*

2 *A pullout cutting board near the cooktop is one of the kitchen's handiest features, allowing the quick transfer of chopped vegetables to a hot pan.*

3 *No cabinet space is lost to corners in the new layout. The island's arc offers additional counter space for working or serving diners who pull up to the ledge with stools. An added patio door enhances kitchen views and makes the outdoors more accessible for entertaining.*

4 *Maple cabinets and a naturally finished wood floor result in plenty of warmth. Cobalt walls and light fixtures lend a modern punch, while stainless fixtures, hardware, and accents contribute to the contemporary feel.*

5 *On one wall, the cabinetry resembles a hutch with a countertop area that's great for serving beverages. Upper doors feature translucent glass inserts with an etched, four-square design.*

1

Lighthearted
Liveliness

A historic house needn't mean a period kitchen. After all, most people aren't interested in going back to ice boxes and coal cookstoves, so any rework of an old kitchen involves considerable updating. For some, that includes style as well as function.

This contemporary kitchen in a circa-1910 house in a historic Atlanta neighborhood is a case in point. Period touches include stained-glass windows and a hutch with vintage proportions and detailing. Everything else gets a contemporary twist: The pantry is paneled in stainless to match the refrigerator, overhead lights number in the dozens, the oak center island is painted black, and mobiles of brightly colored little people flutter from the ceiling.

Look closely, though, and you'll find a well-organized efficiency to the layout that belies the whimsical appearance. The work core is divided into three workstations: a baking alcove, a cooking island, and a cleanup area. Each station has its own appliances and utensils, plus counter materials that correspond to the task performed. Multiple seating areas in the adjacent family room keep friends and family close to the cooking action, but out of the preparation area.

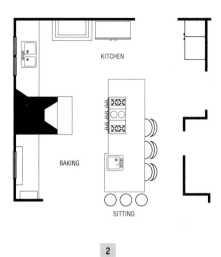

KITCHEN

BAKING

SITTING

2

3

4

1 This playful-looking kitchen is also hardworking: The island, topped with stainless steel, functions as a meal prep and dining surface. The white painted brick fireplace not only provides warm ambience but is used for cooking fish and smoking meat. Baking and cleanup nooks are found on either side.

2 The island seats six for snacking and has a vegetable sink and cooktop. The kitchen's layout provides easy access to the home's dining and family rooms.

3 Tucked between the fireplace and a storage cabinet, stained-glass windows brighten the cleanup area. Granite countertops easily wipe clean; the mottled surface hides the occasional missed crumb.

4 Usually homeowners choose to recase refrigerators in wood to match the cabinetry. Here the opposite approach is taken, cladding the pantry in stainless to match the refrigerator.

5 Side-by-side ovens sit beneath a granite counter in the baking center. Peg-Board keeps bakeware and utensils on display and within arm's reach.

5

During the 1950s, Joseph Eichler, a California contractor, conceived and developed modern-style housing with sun-loving, garden-loving families in mind. The houses became instant classics, and those who own them are reluctant to alter their sleek, open designs.

The problem is, even Eichler's forward-thinking architects never imagined that the kitchen would become part of the family living space. In the house shown here, a load-bearing wall separated the kitchen from the living and dining area, and its only view was through a small, east-facing window. Fifty years later, a plan to include the kitchen in the open, sun-lit living space without violating original design concepts came into focus. Careful planning and a few architectural tricks now make it happen.

2

3 4

1 This round island is the key to the remodeled kitchen's success. Incorporating two posts that support the load-bearing beams above it, the island opens the room to the home's sunny living and dining areas, allows the cook to converse with guests, visually separates the two spaces, and even offers serving and dining space.

2 Speckled granite countertops, maple cabinets, and stainless appliances combine for a streamlined look, respecting the home's original design. Extra-wide windows make the most of views and California sunlight.

3 Glass-and-stainless shelves echo the shape of the island's curves and provide display space for collectible glassware and dishes.

4 A futuristic-looking glass range hood complements the home's style without restricting light or views.

This three-door kitchen in a cozy Tudor house hardly could be described as workable. Swinging portals chopped up the space, blocked the tiny eating table, and made it feel more like a hallway in a boarding house than a family kitchen. A peninsula of nearly floor-to-ceiling cabinets further confined the work area. As far as ambience was concerned, a lonely window located on the shady north side of the house and cold blue painted walls didn't help.

Fortunately the fixes for these problems are fairly simple: Doorways are turned into open passages, the peninsula becomes a breakfast bar, half of a wall is removed, the layout gets a few judicious tweaks, and warm colors and cabinetry brighten the overall mood. The result is a comfy, livable kitchen that's now a pleasure to spend time in.

Coming
Unhinged

Before   **After**

2

3

1 *Distressed, Shaker-style fir cabinets add warmth to the kitchen, as do red painted walls.*

2 *A convenient breakfast bar just 2 feet wide replaces a refrigerator and cabinet wall, opening the work core. Behind the breakfast bar, the upper half of a wall separating the kitchen from a stairwell was removed, visually enlarging the space and bringing in much-needed light.*

3 *A refrigerator, wine rack, and beverage counter, plus some additional storage cabinetry, make efficient use of the corner vacated by the old dining table. Stainless-steel appliances used throughout the kitchen blend well with the neutral tile floors, backsplash, and the granite countertops.*

4 *Setting the new range at an angle in a corner makes it easier than ever to use—and moving it away from the window allows for a range hood. Made from the same edge-grain fir as the cabinets, the new hood is both handsome and unobtrusive.*

5 *The sink's new location takes advantage of the bay window's view— a spot that had unwisely been occupied by the range in the kitchen's previous incarnation. The tumbled marble backsplash tiles and shiny granite countertop reflect the natural light.*

All
Together

When everyone gravitates to the kitchen, as company tends to do, what you really need is space. This Georgian Revival home's kitchen nearly doubled in length for a total of 21 feet, thanks to a bump-out addition. Smart planning makes it function well, allowing everyone to gather and help without getting in each other's way.

A high-functioning island acts as the center anchoring four sides of the kitchen, each a separate zone. The window wall hosts a cleanup zone with a sink and two dishwashers. A professional-style range on another wall creates a cooking zone. The other two quadrants make up a pastry zone and a dining/prep zone.

Roominess and efficiency aside, much of this kitchen's appeal is in its good looks, which complement the home's architecture. Beneath a coffered ceiling, a pot rack hangs over the island; its modern light fixtures feature retrofitted antique, schoolhouse-style shades. The furniture-like island has a teak top, useful for chopping chores. Marble countertops and random-width wood floors blend for a look that is casual, elegant, and hardworking.

1 A dining area connects the enlarged kitchen to the family room. Most casual dining takes place at the kitchen's dining counter so the dining table gets used for everything from homework and games to formal dinners.

2 The cleanup wall features marble counters with drainage grooves near the sink plus two dishwashers. A huge bay window draws light into the kitchen.

3 Tucked alongside the island's sink, a refrigerator drawer holds produce and cheeses. It's a cinch to pull out what's needed, wash it, then slice, dice, or chop right on the island's teak top.

4 The large U-shape kitchen gains efficiency with a multipurpose 7×3-foot island that's as stylish as any piece of furniture. Crafted of cherry with turned legs, bookshelves, basket pullouts, and a teak top, it's a showstopping focal point.

5 The new plan treated the original butler's pantry to a makeover as well. A farmhouse-style sink, new glass cabinet fronts, and a wine cooler share the elegant space, which stores plenty and doubles as a bar during parties. The sink is well-suited to preparing flowers, and the nifty display shelf keeps small items out of deep cabinets.

Small Moves for
Big Change

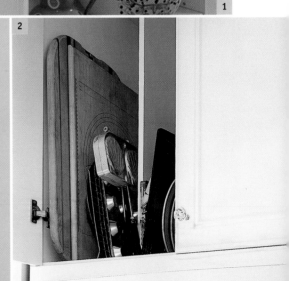

1 Lengthening the counter into a broad peninsula creates a comfy place for guests to join the cook. A drawer to the side contains flatware and napkins for countertop dining.

2 Vertical dividers create ideal storage for cutting boards and bakeware in the cabinet over the wall oven.

3 No fronts, glass fronts, and full fronts add variety to the cabinetry. The ridged metal "EAT" piece on the range hood turns the cooking center into a lively focal point. Shallow display shelving ends the peninsula. A checkerboard of black and white floor tiles adds verve to the overall look.

4 Paring back the walls that separated the kitchen from the back entry opens up the space. The back entry's formerly blank wall spaces are now lined with pantry cupboards.

This kitchen broke out of its cramped configuration with three smart changes: A built-in cabinet next to the refrigerator makes way for a wall oven and smarter storage; a window bump-out over the sink provides display space and natural light; and shortening a wall from the back entry draws that space into the kitchen. Though the kitchen's original, standing-room-only size remains the same, the space appears and lives larger.

One important change involved the ceiling. Removing the suspended ceiling boosts the room height to 9½ feet. Another subtlety that adds to a more spacious whole: One end of the countertop bends into a peninsula, allowing the cook to talk with guests and prepare food at the same time. The kitchen's lively, graphic decor conveys a mastery of scale: Bold checkerboard floor tiles give the space visual punch and draw out the wallpaper's veggie details. White cabinets make a clean backdrop against which dishware and collectibles are displayed.

3

Before

After

4

Classic
Craftsman

This 1909 craftsman-style house had fulfilled its role as a boarding house since World War II. As a result, the kitchen area in particular suffered from fragmentation. Its red and white cabinets didn't match the craftsman colors in the rest of the house, and a rear porch isolated the room from backyard views. The kitchen needed architectural help to pull itself together and become the hub of a single-family home.

That help came in the form of both style and function. Stylewise, craftsman materials, surfaces, and design themes now pop up throughout the room. Functionally, the porch is now used as a breakfast room with great backyard views. The room functions better than ever, thanks to a 48-inch commercial range, a generous work island, an abundance of natural and artificial light, and a clear division between gathering and eating areas and the spacious, well-organized work core.

4

Linoleum *Makes a Comeback*

In this kitchen overhaul, linoleum was used for the floor—a choice that's regaining popularity. Though the material's prevalence never waned in Europe, sales in this country suffered after vinyl flooring was introduced in the 1970s. Chic again due to its design flexibility, lower cost to value, environmentally friendly ingredients, and durability, linoleum is once again moving from commercial applications into residences across the United States.

Why is it a wise flooring choice? Linoleum floors don't release harmful gases, or VOCs (volatile organic compounds), and because the linseed oil in linoleum is constantly oxidizing, it retards the growth of bacteria. (The recipe for linoleum includes linseed oil, crushed limestone, wood shavings, and pine resin tapped from living trees.) The fact that linoleum actually hardens over time is yet another plus.

Linoleum is available in a dazzling array of colors and is flexible enough for you to cut it into original designs, such as the bow-tie pattern on this kitchen floor. It costs $4 to $5 per square foot installed, double the price of high-end vinyl sheet flooring, but several dollars less than hardwood flooring.

1 *A farmhouse sink with a swing faucet has a nostalgic look—and makes filling big pots and washing large pans and serving pieces easy.*

2 *The ample island offers a surface for baking or snacking, a second sink, and open shelves at one end for storing cookware. Designed to look like a craftsman-style library table, the island features a base of quartersawn oak and a top of maple butcher block. The room's craftsman details include geometric backsplash tiles, squared-off light fixtures, painted cabinets with recessed panels, and a linoleum floor. A blackboard—great for making grocery lists or taking phone messages—covers the built-in fridge.*

3 *Saucepans and frying pans hang on a rack in the corner between windows where they won't obscure the views or light.*

4 *The breakfast area, two steps down from the kitchen, features a built-in bench with a table and a pass-through to the hutch.*

85

Universal Design

Ease for All

Universal design makes a house more livable and functional for people of all ages and abilities. Many homeowners are incorporating universal design concepts into their homes whether or not they need them right away. The kitchen featured here applies a host of universal design principles.

Good looks. No matter how accommodating a kitchen is, if it doesn't look good, you'll resist using it.

Comfortable reach. Locate door handles, appliances, electrical switches, and outlets 15 to 48 inches above the floor. That way, anyone can reach them comfortably.

Aisles and approach room. You'll need 48-inch aisles—which is often recommended for multicook kitchens—and 60 inches of space for wheelchair turnaround.

Cooking appliances. Wall ovens and separate cooktops with pull-up space beneath are the safest way to go. Select front-mounted controls for easy access.

Knee clearances, toe-kicks. Wheelchair users require knee clearances of 27 inches high, 30 inches wide, and 19 inches deep. Similarly extra-large 9×6-inch toe-kicks allow chair users to pull up closer. Some cabinet manufacturers offer such toe-kicks as an option when you order; you can modify other cabinets.

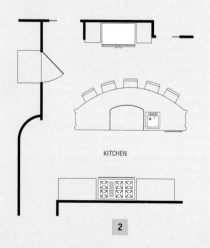

KITCHEN

Cabinetry. Choose finishes that tend to hide dings and marks.

Handles. The longer, the better. Some stylish handles even run the full length of a cabinet.

Faucets. Hands-free faucets that turn on with a sensor are becoming more readily available for home use. Faucets that are mounted to the side, rather than the back, of sinks eliminate long reaches.

Storage. Plot lots of storage in lower cabinets; fit them with pullout shelves for dishes, pots, and pans.

Counter space. Put ample stretches of countertop wherever possible, especially next to the refrigerator, oven, stove, and sink.

Floors and thresholds. Choose a material that's firm and smooth. Eliminate bumpy thresholds.

Countertops. Bullnose fronts and rounded corners reduce injury and help those who use a wheelchair "shove off" from a counter, using just an elbow or forearm.

[1] *It's wise to place a microwave fairly low, no matter the age or ability of those who use it: The higher you must reach to remove a hot item, the greater the chance of spilling it—and potential burns. The cook in this home insisted on a pro-style range with front-mounted controls. The oven is accessible because nothing impedes a wheelchair on either side, and countertops provide quick landing spots for dishes hot from the oven.*

[2] *Placing the refrigerator close to the pantry with counter space between simplifies the chore of putting away groceries. For easy access, the pantry has a pocket door instead of the standard swing style. A large kitchen island allows multiple cooks of various physical capabilities to work together. Where a peninsula would "trap" the cooks, an island always provides an alternative route.*

[3] *Lots of storage in lower cabinets creates easy access for all, including small children.*

[4] *Supply lines for both the main sink and dropped-level prep sink are housed in the cabinetry to avoid burns.*

1

From the Gut-Go

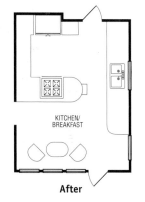

After

KITCHEN/
BREAKFAST

Sometimes you have to make drastic changes in order to get what you want. In this 1905 kitchen in California, the only original element is the pine floor—and even that has been refinished.

Saddled with trying to fulfill too many needs and plagued with a lack of light, the kitchen became crowded with problems: a space-gobbling laundry nook; a mid-room island; an intrusive range hood; a superfluous, traffic-stopping bathroom door; plus dark, dated paneling and cabinetry, and tiny windows.

The remodel started with the addition of a wall of windows, revealing a wonderful view of the garden and inviting lots of light into the room. Though modestly proportioned, the room now feels so much bigger that an addition becomes unnecessary. The windows also eliminate the need for a range hood. Now the cook simply throws open a window to vent cooking odors (this is California, remember!). Wood cabinetry made of ash—a light, warm

wood—and rounded cabinet and counter corners make the room feel bigger and eliminate the hazards of sharp edges.

Tackling each problem one at a time, the laundry nook is relocated to the second floor, the bathroom door is sealed off (the bath is still accessible from the dining room), and a pocket door replaces a swinging door to the dining room, freeing up more space. Finally, a peninsula forms a natural barrier between the dining area and the cook's turf, replacing the obtrusive island and making entertaining easier. The new peninsula doesn't require as much clearance as a freestanding island and provides plenty of counter space and a home for the range.

Color *without* Paint

If the thought of painting over the beautiful grain on your new natural wood cabinetry makes you faint, but you would still like to inject a shot of color—or colors—to your kitchen, consider dyeing some of the wood. Daring blocks of red-, yellow-, and blue-dyed ash drawer fronts in this kitchen *right* surround the stainless-steel-and-black oven in the peninsula. Aniline dye, available at hardware stores and home improvement centers, stains the wood with deep, rich colors but allows the grain to show through. In this kitchen, the stained drawer fronts all were cut from the same board, so the grain pattern runs behind all three colors, enhancing the effect.

2

3 4

1 *Plenty of light streams into this kitchen through large new windows and an existing skylight. The sunshine plays off the blonde wood cabinets and refinished pine floor. Waves of ocean-green granite provide a glossy contrast to the ash cabinets. The rounded corners of the countertops add the illusion of increased square footage.*

2 *Aniline dye—in red, yellow, and blue—gives the cabinet drawer fronts surrounding the oven a jolt of color.*

3 *An 8-foot-tall wall of windows makes dining in this kitchen feel like an outdoor event. Fixed windows above and below the operable casements give the windows a sense of proportion.*

4 *Rounded ash shelves create the perfect spot for displaying collectibles. Sandblasted green glass provides translucent cover for everyday dishes.*

89

You may be able to gain the space you need to expand a too-small kitchen without the expense and disruption of building an addition. By annexing space from an adjoining pantry and den, the kitchen in this Illinois farmhouse gained 60 square feet and a vastly more efficient layout without moving an exterior wall.

Finding more space inside, rather than outside, your home works particularly well when the rooms that surround your kitchen are part of the problem. In this case, one had to walk through the pantry to reach the staircase, which meant much of the pantry was off-limits for storage. Because the pantry also made room for the refrigerator (inconveniently located outside of the kitchen), traffic came to a halt whenever someone opened the appliance door.

The new design pushes the kitchen wall back to the stairway and adds a peninsula that functions both as a breakfast bar and much-needed counter space. A smaller but more efficient walk-in pantry stores everything the old hallway did and more—without putting it on view to stairway traffic. Finally, the fridge now has a place in the kitchen proper, just steps away from the peninsula, the cooking area, and the sink, creating an efficient work triangle.

The other changes were both aesthetic and functional. Enlarged windows allow for more natural light and a better view of the backyard. A columned half-wall, once a full wall separating the kitchen and dining area, increases the sense of space and creates a handy pass-through.

A Built-in Addition

1

2

Before

After

3

4

1 The removal of interior walls that separated this kitchen from adjoining rooms made space for a peninsula that doubles as a breakfast bar. Shaker-style cabinets with vintage-looking brass pulls and seeded-glass inserts respect the origins of the 18th-century Midwestern farmhouse in which this kitchen resides.

2 This kitchen gained square footage and efficiency without the expense of a full addition. Instead it claimed poorly and little-used space from rooms around it. If you want to gain space for your own kitchen, walk the perimeter of the original footprint and hunt for underused nooks and crannies to rework.

3 Simple pendant lamps illuminate the granite-top peninsula. The louvered door on the back wall leads to a stairway and lower level. Beaded board capped with molding creates an inconspicuous shelf for artwork.

4 The half-wall and classic column that separate the kitchen from the dining room add handsome woodwork, historic detail, and a sense of space. On a practical level, the "window" serves as a pass-through from kitchen to dining area.

91

Stay Awhile
Space

Two easy moves stretched the footprint of this now-gracious kitchen, making room for desired spaces, styles, and activities. The first closed off one of two entries to a back stairwell; the second reconfigured the kitchen's breakfast nook, transitioning the nook and a tiny laundry/entry combo into a powder room and a roomier laundry area.

The kitchen itself was remodeled with serious cooking and frequent gathering in mind. The closed-off entry now permits an uninterrupted L-shape layout, supplemented by a long, table-height island. From the kitchen's entry the island appears as a table, with drawers for cutlery and napkins and comfy chairs pulled up. On the work core side, cabinets under the island conceal a plethora of cooking equipment. The island's size is generous, making room for friends who sit for coffee while bread's being baked, and children who do homework and chat with parents. Now there's plenty of room for everyone.

Continued on page 94

1 Commercial-grade appliances in stainless steel add a crisp note to the remodeled kitchen's warm, woodsy style. The island is topped in maple butcher block; cabinets are oil-finished cherry. Butter-yellow walls and trim complement wine-red window sashes.

2 Opposite the kitchen's "L," a microwave oven tucks behind a sliding door. A pullout ledge beneath it serves as a landing spot. A roomy pantry with broad, shallow drawers for linens and trays, a countertop for food preparation, and glass-fronted upper cabinets that showcase glassware and fine china both serve and beautify.

3 Open shelves put pretty dishware on display and contribute to the new kitchen's relaxed, welcoming ambience. A slim, wall-mounted ledge and accompanying stool create a telephone center.

93

Before

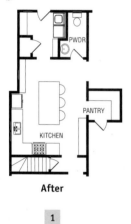

After

1

2

1 *With dine-in seating moved to the kitchen, nobody mourned the loss of the old breakfast nook. The move made it possible to open the kitchen to a new family space, formerly a big porch.*

2 *The reworked and widened mudroom/laundry benefits from the previous kitchen's cabinets. A new pocket door separates it from the kitchen and provides better access to the small room than did the old swinging door.*

3 *Closing off a second basement entry made room for a tight, L-shape work core and plenty of wall space for cabinets. Cabinets tuck under the island's butcher-block surface but do not run its entire perimeter, so from one side the island looks more like a large table.*

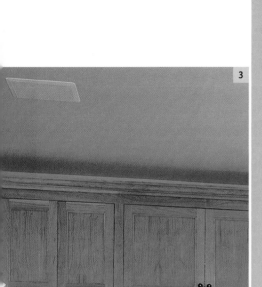

How *High?*

The 30-inch-tall island in this kitchen reaches table height, making it ideal for the rolling and kneading that go with baking, as well as for seated dining. If that height and those activities appeal to you, go for it. Keep in mind, though, that a 30-inch height is too low to accommodate a sink or oven.

Most islands are 36 inches tall, but many incorporate bar-height ledges at 42 inches to make room for stool-sitters and bar-leaners. These hiked-up ledges also serve to visually and physically separate the island's eating area from its work core.

Standard countertop height is also 36 inches, so it's no coincidence that appliances such as dishwashers and ranges are built to slip under this height. If you're a taller person and want a 38- or 39-inch counter height, you can have a base made to raise an appliance.

Sit-down desks are generally built at 30-inch heights. Give this some thought in your planning: If the desk is a telephone cabinet, work space, or shelf that you will primarily use when standing, build it at 42 inches to enjoy stand-up comfort.

From Age-Old to
Vintage Modern

1

Don't let this kitchen's vintage charm fool you: It has the ambience of yesteryear, but its function is thoroughly modern. Moreover, most of its elements are brand new.

The kitchen is part of a 1910 Portland, Oregon, house that had little going for it but plenty of space. Nothing had been done to bring it up to date: When the new homeowner arrived, she found a stove, a sink, a fridge, and one countertop in the butler's pantry. To bring this kitchen into the 21st century, yet maintain the vintage look the homeowner

desired, much work had to be done. First the back porch and butler's pantry had to join the kitchen's floor plan. From there, three centers emerge: the primary prep, cook, and cleanup area; the refrigerator and secondary work center; and the dining area. Finally, the new kitchen is dressed in vintage-look elements that, thanks to modern technology, function far better than their earlier counterparts.

2

Before

After

1 An old, refurbished white range underscores the vintage charm of this kitchen, but that's the only element that is truly old. The deep farmhouse sink with wall-mounted faucet is new, as are the vinyl tile flooring and the aluminum-edge linoleum countertops. Most of the kitchen's primary prep, cook, and cleanup area was once a large-but-inefficient butler's pantry.

2 A vintage floral-motif apron, attached to the cabinet opening with hook-and-loop tape, conceals a doggie door between the kitchen's exterior wall and the outdoors.

3 No more headfirst dives beneath the sink: Emptying the trash and finding cleaning supplies is a cinch with this ingenious pullout cabinet.

4 The refrigerator anchors a second work area, which doubles as a beverage center. A stretch of countertop, plus a small sink, wine rack, and glassware shelving, create a hardworking corner.

Commercial Class

One of the most significant kitchen trends in recent years has been the migration of commercial-grade products and materials into residential kitchens. Professional chefs have long enjoyed the benefits of high-powered burners, dual-fuel ranges, easy-to-clean stainless appliances, and cool, smooth stone-slab work surfaces for rolling dough. Today, commercial-grade appliances and materials are increasingly available at retail outlets, making it easy for anyone to incorporate these features into a kitchen.

The trend goes beyond function: Commercial kitchens have become a full-blown aesthetic that celebrates high-quality industrial materials, sleek surfaces, and rugged good looks. Manufacturers of consumer-grade products are following suit, cladding home appliances in commercial-look surfaces. Meanwhile inventive homeowners are finding ways to repurpose commercial products, such as shelving and storage units, and industrial materials, including galvanized steel, glass slabs, and concrete, in creative ways to enhance both the function and the form of their kitchens. Use the following examples to inspire and incorporate commercial style into your kitchen.

1 A cabinet with a glass-slab top, a set of stainless canisters, commercial-grade shelves, and frosted-glass cabinet doors give this corner of this kitchen an apothecarylike feel.

2 A couple of roll-away mechanic tool cabinets tuck under each end of this copper-top island to provide moveable storage as well as additional work surfaces. The top of one cabinet is fitted with a butcher block for chopping; the other features a slab of granite for baking-related tasks. Both have sturdy, smooth-gliding drawers perfect for storing cooking implements and small appliances. The cabinets' red, black, and silver color scheme matches that of the rest of the kitchen.

3 An engine-turned, stainless-steel backsplash and high-gloss, yellow-lacquer cabinetry more than catch your eye. This kitchen has the modernistic look of a high-style, contemporary office or factory. Lab-gray laminate clads lower cabinets and appliances with a muted matte finish, a soothing contrast to the glitter and gloss.

4 On the softer side, commercial style can be subtle too. In this kitchen, it takes the form of an exposed granite backsplash wall, full-width stainless-steel drawer pulls, and sleek linear metal-clad appliances.

Two Takes

The Arts and Crafts style, also known as craftsman or Mission style, was a solid and simple reaction to Victorian frippery and excess. It took the design world by storm with its rugged, handsome linear shapes and the flamelike grain of quarter sawn oak in the early 1900s, reaching its peak popularity in the 1920s before giving way to Art Deco. The style is enjoying renewed popularity today: Its heretofore undervalued charms and emphasis on clean lines and natural materials make this style a shoe-in for a modern aesthetic.

Trouble is, while Arts and Crafts living and dining rooms feature oak trim, cozy inglenooks, and elegant built-ins, kitchens in such houses usually remained cold and utilitarian.

Continued on page 102

1| This remodeled kitchen in an Arts and Crafts vintage home almost looks like it has been there all along. New Mission-style cabinets stop short of the ceiling for an unfitted look. Rolled-glass panes on the cabinet doors exude an impression of age. The new island, made of quartersawn, fumed oak topped with luna-moth-blue ceramic tile, looks like a piece of vintage furniture, yet houses a commercial cooktop and oven.

2| Arts and Crafts houses typically cloister kitchens. This kitchen's renovation opened sight lines into the dining room, creating a need for design consistency from room to room. Treating the kitchen cabinets with the same dark finish and iron hardware used on the antique furnishings in the adjoining room helped the kitchen flow into the home's more formal spaces.

3| Full-faced drawers such as these are usually reserved for fine furniture, so they are a welcome surprise behind the kitchen's base-cabinet doors.

4| Hand-forged iron pulls with a hammered finish are as hefty and authentic-looking as the solid oak doors they adorn.

1

1 This kitchen takes simple, strong Arts and Crafts lines and improvises on a theme, changing cabinet colors from dark oak to red.

2 Granite wasn't used in vintage Arts and Crafts homes, but its heft and natural origins fit the aesthetic. The crystalline gray of this particular stone blends well with vintage-style chrome faucets and stainless-steel sinks.

3 Recycled blue glass inserts reminiscent of Arts and Crafts-style tile treatments adorn the granite backsplash. Blue was chosen as an accent color to complement the red stained cabinets.

4 A lack of natural light proved to be a major concern in this kitchen. A solution: Upper cabinets backed by frosted-glass windows and fitted with reeded-glass doors not only admit daylight but highlight the collectibles stored inside.

An Arts and Crafts-style kitchen simply did not exist. That said, there's no reason you can't create one now, as the two kitchens shown here and on pages 100 and 101 prove. The first carries the Arts and Crafts style of a vintage home into the kitchen, while the second uses the style's themes as a starting point for an elegant redo.

Sometimes you need to start from scratch to get the space, layout, or amenities you want. If you're building a new house, you have the luxury of a clean slate and a no-limits design that truly suits the way your family cooks, gathers, and entertains. On the other hand if you're remodeling, and prepared to gut and rebuild your kitchen from the floor up, you can enjoy similar benefits. Think full additions and soaring ceilings—both are doable and bring great gains in livability, style, and hardworking function. Although large remodeling projects are expensive, the cost of building a new kitchen often is a bargain compared to trading up to a larger home. And doing so is a more attractive option if the rest of your house and neighborhood is to your liking. The pages that follow contain a gallery of inspiring possibilities you will want to consider.

See page 131

See page 132

Make
New

The Enlightened Kitchen

This kitchen began life as a 9×11-foot galley at the end of a 1950s ranch. Topping its list of troubles, it was too small and far too dark—especially for its cloudy Portland,

Oregon, climate, where residents welcome and savor every bit of natural light.

A major kitchen addition and overhaul pushed out the back walls of the kitchen and adjacent dining room 8½ feet and replaced the flat 8-foot ceiling with a dramatic vault. To invite in as much light as possible, a large picture window flanked by two casement windows stretches nearly the entire length of the 18-foot south wall. High above the room's A-frame truss, a clerestory window draws

Before

After

even more light to the space. Reeded-glass pocket doors share the kitchen's sunshine with the dining room, even when the doors are closed.

The new kitchen's materials are warm in feel too. The cabinets of indigenous Oregon woods with hand-rubbed oil and glazed paint finishes blend with the honey-hue granite countertops.

1 A ceiling of tongue-and-groove fir vaults to a height of 14 feet, making the room seem ultraspacious. Artificial light abounds, from pressed-tin cones that focus on the 8×5-foot island to halogen lights that descend from cables strung above the countertops. Storage under the island, in lower cabinets, and in a wall pantry keeps the need for upper cabinets to a minimum, allowing for the 18-foot window overlooking a wooded valley. The cabinets and island top are white oak.

2 Lower cabinets are painted with a hand-mixed, multicolored glaze finish that echoes the hues and variegation in the granite countertops. The same white oak floors in the kitchen continue throughout the house.

3 Bookshelves, cubbyholes for wine, and a small work area fit snugly between the refrigerator and pantry on the wall opposite the windows.

4 The 5×8-foot island serves food prep and homework needs. Wide planks of white oak, their natural checks and cracks left unmasked, lend warmth, character, and detail to the large surface.

1

Into the Light

This kitchen, which overlooks Puget Sound and the Olympic Mountains, relishes one of the country's great views. But it wasn't always so. Formerly the house squinted at that vista through two tiny windows above the sink. Furthermore, a prime south-facing location went to waste—it didn't take advantage of precious Northwestern sunshine and natural light.

For this home, an addition was the only way to overcome these deficiencies, and it paid off in spades, creating a light-filled living, working, food preparation, and eating area in the back of the 1940s colonial-style house.

Key to the project's success is a sizable island located in the center of the work area. Not only does the island make for an efficient layout and plenty of counter space, its huge storage capacity kept the need for upper cabinets to a minimum, making way for light-gathering, view-inspired windows on three sides of the added space.

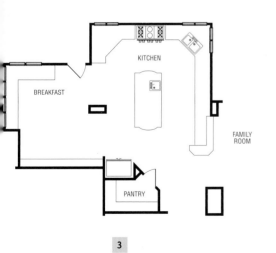

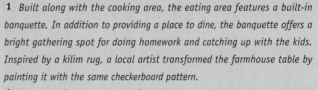

1 Built along with the cooking area, the eating area features a built-in banquette. In addition to providing a place to dine, the banquette offers a bright gathering spot for doing homework and catching up with the kids. Inspired by a kilim rug, a local artist transformed the farmhouse table by painting it with the same checkerboard pattern.

2 Two sets of corner windows flank the new stainless-steel range, providing the cook with daylight and dazzling views. The divided-light casement windows echo the style of other windows in the 60-year-old house and blur the distinction between it and the addition.

3 An elongated island is the hub of the cooking area. A 42-inch-high countertop loosely connects the kitchen to the adjacent family room.

KITCHEN

BREAKFAST

FAMILY
ROOM

PANTRY

1

2

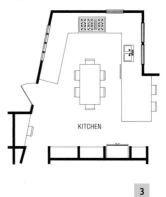

Uptown
Country

This brand-new kitchen—part cutting-edge styling, part cozy country—simply can't get enough Colorado sunshine. Designers purposely made the footprint big enough to allow glass on three sides of the kitchen. Then they filled it up with windows: glass block undercabinet walls, double-hung windows, and traditional windows in vaulted spaces. To boost collection display capabilities, the limestone countertop is 32 inches deep—6 inches deeper than standard—creating a ledge for pottery, plants, oils, and spices. White glass-fronted upper cabinets reflect light and seem to float between the vaulted ceiling and glass block; the green painted lowers add warmth near the pine floor.

KITCHEN

3

Country *on Edge*

This kitchen is a terrific example of how a design can combine contemporary and country aesthetics. The strategy is point-counterpoint: For every edgy aspect, something soft and familiar has a place. When equally blended, the two looks keep each other from appearing too cold or too soft. In this kitchen:

- A high-tech refrigerator adopts wood-panel doors.
- Copper pots hang from an ultra simple—not rustic—pot rack.
- A modern limestone-and-steel range hood is accented with rusty bolt heads and pottery.
- A sleek stainless-steel range is flanked by green painted lower cabinets.
- Glass blocks and traditional double-hung windows draw in lots of light.

4

5

1 *The tall peninsula hosts casual dining and also conceals kitchen messes from the dining area. Inside the kitchen, a table functions as an island. The ceiling treatment is two-fold: Vaulted space hovers over the range and a curved, contemporary wood-grain veneer decorates the lower interior ceiling.*

2 *This Colorado country home is a contemporary take on a farm building. Beneath a tall, sloping roofline, the kitchen juts out from the main house. A combination of traditional windows and a row of glass blocks draws light into the space.*

3 *The basic U-shape allows for long stretches of counter space, which is great for food prep and entertaining.*

4 *A row of glass blocks creates unique display opportunities and draws in shots of sunlight.*

5 *A planning area tucks into a far corner near the kitchen's exterior entrance. Cookbooks and household office supplies fill the shelves and drawers.*

6 *Paneled doors blend the refrigerator and the storage wall, which includes a counter and shelves that make up a beverage center. Guests needn't go deep into the kitchen to help themselves.*

6

Grand
Tradition

Previous remodeling jobs and wall demolitions left the kitchen of this 1889 house with plenty of room to expand. The idea was to make the kitchen into a place where cooks and guests can enjoy each other's company in style while meal prep is underway. The floor plan rotated 90 degrees to make room for an efficient work core as well as an ample gathering place for guests.

Although entirely new, the room features a traditional look, quality materials, and detailing and scale appropriate to the home's 19th-century architecture. The elements reach into the past: rich cherry cabinetry, deep moldings, a foil of light-color backsplash tiles, creamy speckled granite counters, and inset hardwood floors. The elegant result is similar to that of a Victorian library.

1 An arched-top window edged with deep, beveled trim graciously frames the sunlit view. A double light fixture over the sink illuminates the work area in proportion to the room's grand scale.

2 Knocking out a wall, pantry, and powder room enabled this kitchen to double in size. Behind the wet bar, a concealed washer and dryer are stacked in a closet.

3 This hutch, composed of cabinetry pieces, features a dark stained upper cabinet set over a cherry base.

4 Thanks to a tight work core, hot pans straight from the oven find a place quickly on the island or countertop. Sophisticated and sociable, this island with a cooktop keeps a cooking host in touch with visitors, who pull up stools to chat. The island's furniture styling includes turned legs and bun feet; the stools' black leather seats feature nailhead trim.

5 A tall, glass-fronted hutch holds enough glassware for large parties at this cocktail bar, which also features a sink and undercabinet storage.

6 Two classic floor borders encircle the island and kitchen perimeter. Each is crafted of mahogany and Peruvian walnut strips set in a field of oak.

4

5

6

Before

1

2

3

4

While 10×13 feet is plenty of floor space for an efficiently designed kitchen, this case features a 1941 arrangement that was too cramped. The solution was to stretch the kitchen, extending the space with a 7-foot bump-out addition to the front of the home. The bump-out produced enough room to draw the refrigerator into the heart of the kitchen and to add a prep sink and numerous storage-smart cabinets, all topped with a run of much-needed counter space.

Cabinetry, hardware, and reproduction light fixtures over the sink keep up with the home's 1940s architecture. The lighting scheme, comprised of a ceiling fixture, under-cabinet task lighting, and reproduction fixtures at the sink, amply light the room no matter the hour. The new surfaces—hardwood, granite, and tile—make cleanup a snap.

Give It a
Stretch

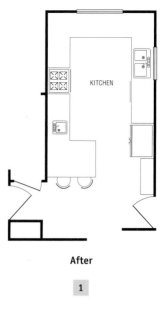

After

1

1 The kitchen's floor plan gained 70 square feet and received much-needed cabinet and counter space and a second sink. A short peninsula with two stools lets friends and family visit with the cooks but keeps them out of the meal prep area.

2 The kitchen's new, longer footprint makes room for a continuous wrap of granite countertop. The pretty yellow and white color scheme—a few shades lighter than the colors it replaced—blends with the home's overall palette.

3 The main sink is located beneath a window that shows off a garden view.

4 In the food prep area, broad drawers are fitted with stepped dividers to keep spices handy and visible.

5 Note the prep sink to the left of the range, an indispensible element in a two-cook kitchen. The tile shelf above the range keeps counter clutter to a minimum.

6 Pullout shelves in a cupboard across from the peninsula store pantry items and cookbooks.

115

Room for Everyone

1

Before

After

2

This space rarely rests, accommodating the activities of a large extended family whose members like to get together for everything from huge family dinners and late-night feedings to early morning snacks and midday naps.

The kitchen's layout looks simple—and it is—but it took some major reorientation to make it so. Relocating the basement stairwell and dropping walls between the kitchen and dining room opened the space, making room for a table-backed island that visually separates the kitchen from the dining room.

The new kitchen features three distinct zones: cleanup, food prep,

and comfort (a cushioned corner window seat). Cooking for a crowd takes place at the high-powered dual-fuel range fitted with an electric oven, six gas burners, and a gas broiler. A pot-filler mounts above the range, and a warming drawer to the side saves portions for those who can't make dinner with the rest of the family. To maximize refrigerator space, the full-size refrigerator is entirely devoted to cool—not frozen—storage. Two freezer drawers on the island store ice cream and a few days' worth of frozen items, and a chest freezer in a nearby utility room handles the big freezer load.

1 A mix of materials creates a homey kitchen that's durable and easy on the eyes. A clean-lined arrangement of soft yellow walls, metallic tiles, slate countertops, buttery paneled cabinets, pretty fabrics, and professional-grade appliances blends well to convey comfort.

2 Taking down walls to better orient this kitchen to the dining area made it more family-friendly and efficient. It created views from one space to another, allowing spectacular outdoor vistas from nearly any location on the floor.

3 The island's crescent-shape dining table is an ingenious move that promotes togetherness. It's the site for meals caught on the run, and an appropriate place to pull up a high chair and feed the little ones.

4 Family members can curl up on the window cushion with a book; toddlers use the nook to take a nap.

Refine and Repeat

Old houses often boast rich architecture throughout their living spaces, but their kitchens do not always follow suit. The older kitchen's unadorned, utilitarian nature reflects the fact that people once viewed kitchens as work spaces, not places for family and friends to gather and live in. Such was the case prior to this home's remodeling: The main living areas were spacious, airy, and rich with architectural detail while the dimly lit kitchen, back porch, and mudroom suffered from a dowdy design devoid of pretty views.

The new kitchen accommodates the homeowners' desire to both prepare meals and entertain within its boundaries. While its new look is as elegant as the rest of the 1920s house, the kitchen includes a number of contemporary touches that enliven the space and transform it into an inviting blend of old and new.

In its original form, unattractive cabinets and a dropped ceiling confined the cook. A narrow passage led to a sunroom with views unavailable to those in the kitchen. To reach the backyard, homeowners crossed a

glassed-in porch cluttered with coats and boxes.

The new design annexes a breakfast area and porch, creating a spacious L-shape kitchen that elegantly flows with room for multiple cooks and guests. To achieve this flow, walls were dropped and the kitchen's main work center relocated to the former breakfast room. The original kitchen has become a secondary work center with ovens and its own prep sink. A beverage center claims a wedge of space next to the refrigerator. It consists of a wine rack, a small countertop, and some shelves. Behind, a shallow broom closet goes unnoticed. The once-grungy back porch shines as a light-filled dining area, pantry, and mudroom.

Continued on page 120

Before

After

1 *A color scheme of butter yellow and deep sage complements the warm tones of the cabinetry and hardwood floors. The cleanup zone features a sink, a slim stainless dishwasher, and a mottled amber glass pendant light. The simple lines of the cabinets—some with flat fronts, some with recessed panels, and some with glass fronts—bridge the divide between contemporary and traditional styles.*

2 *The contoured vent hood introduces a curve. Behind it, an arched wall of glass block replaces traditional windows. For a double-diffuse light effect, cupboards that overlap the block feature pebbled-glass fronts and backs.*

119

Theme and Repeat Several traditional and contemporary design themes create a pleasing tension in this kitchen. The strategy at work here is the repeat, and it coordinates rather than disjoints the theme. Not only does repeating a theme insinuate intention, it also boosts the visual impact of a design move. One gentle arch might be amusing in this kitchen, but its repetition—in the range hood, the glass-block window, the cabinet hardware, and the rugs—amplifies its effect. Where crown molding might look gracious but out of place over cabinet tops, its repetition at the wall-ceiling juncture ensures its intention and heightens the effect. Even the liveliness of the glass blocks' wavy texture is echoed in the pebbled-glass cabinet fronts and backs. The lesson? If you want to do something interesting in a space, do it more than once.

1 In a nifty textural move, the backsplash is a checkerboard of glass tiles. They're all the same sage hue, but some have a matte finish, while others are glossy.

2 To create a half-moon table, the kitchen's deep black-red granite countertop travels around the corner in a semicircle. A steel post, which complements the stainless appliances, supports the surface. Diners carry on conversations with the cooks and enjoy garden views simultaneously. An amber pendant illuminates the space. Roll-up matchstick blinds add a touch of natural material to one window while blocking the sun's glare when needed.

Modern, Not Minimalist

Warm woods, lustrous colors, and inviting hues make this sleek, contemporary kitchen/dining area feel as welcoming as the 1930s Tudor home in which it resides. The entire area is a 20×40-foot addition to the back of the home. The soaring 11- and 16-foot ceilings surprise guests, who can't see the addition from the street. The new space has plenty of room for two cooks, family, and friends. The dining room addition comfortably accommodates up to 12 people.

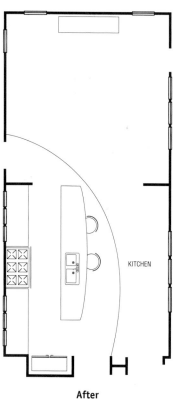

After

KITCHEN

1 *The dining area addition makes room for larger gatherings in a cheerful atmosphere. High-tech lighting joins vintage posters and furnishings with clean traditional lines. Roman shades mounted on ceiling-high windows provide privacy when needed.*

2 *A slim brass strip divides the kitchen's linoleum floor from the dining room's parquet. The strip's curve follows that of the island overhang.*

3 *Grounded by stainless steel, darker furnishings, and iron stools, this kitchen gets its warmth from light maple cabinetry and flooring, multicolor granite countertops, and buttery walls and lighting fixtures.*

4 *Reeded-glass inserts on some drawer fronts break up an otherwise overwhelming mass of wood. They also reveal drawer contents at a glance. Long stainless handles add architectural detail to the sleek cabinetry.*

5 *The pullout faucet's wand switches from flow to spray and is handy for washing or filling deep pots.*

Ahead to
The '60s.

1

All steel and glass, the original kitchen in this 1964 concrete basalt block house proved edgy—and cold and a little cramped. Not a warm, welcoming space for serving family and frequent guests. The solution is a vibrant, earthy palette; a revised floor plan that reaches into the existing living area; and a high-style design that celebrates the home's era.

A granite countertop led the palette's development. The stone features a warm mix of red, pink, and yellow hues. Complementing that mix of colors, yellow, orange, and red-brown make up the palette for this kitchen redesign. A patchwork motif that recalls popular '60s patterns decorates the backsplash and island face.

The new floor plan shortened a wall by the refrigerator, removed a steel beam, and trimmed the peninsula that jutted from the sink wall. Doing so further opened the kitchen to the adjacent living area and made room for a curved, bilevel island around which family and friends gather to dine. The new kitchen handles family life as easily as it does parties of two-dozen guests.

1 This kitchen's vivid palette of earthy hues and stainless steel—rendered in cabinets, tiles, light fixtures, and barstools—helps set the tone for a '60s aura. Cabinet pulls and a unique, sprawling lighting fixture emphasize the room's gentle curves.

2 The window wall brightens the kitchen's primary work zone, an L-shape section containing the stove, microwave, and refrigerator.

3 The curved track lighting and adjustable fixtures are ideal for the concrete ceiling, which doesn't allow the installation of recessed can lighting.

4 A backsplash-to-ceiling window draws in outdoor views. The window's top edge matches that of the cabinets for a streamlined look. Abstract drawer pulls add variety to the hardware mix.

5 The new island is also a full-fledged secondary work space and entertaining center. It houses a wine fridge, small sink, icemaker, and even a two-burner cooktop for whipping up quick appetizers.

Before   5   After

125

Behind Closed Drawers

Storage is one of the kitchen's most important functions because there's so much kitchen stuff to stash away: perishable and nonperishable food items, tableware, pots and pans, cooking utensils, small appliances, cookbooks, and more. The right amount, right kind, and, perhaps most significant, the right placement of storage are central to an efficient kitchen that's a pleasure to work in.

1 Carefully spaced dowels attached to the drawer's bottom keep items from sliding around when the drawer is opened and shut.

2 Hook-and-rack systems for holding pots and pans have been around for a long time. Now the concept has been adapted to store smaller utensils along the backsplash, keeping them at hand and freeing up drawer space.

3 Extra-deep countertops offer additional work space but also make retrieving items in the back of the extra-deep cabinets below a chore. The solution: a unit that resembles a standard cabinet drawer but instead glides all the way out, providing easy access to a heavy mixer. An interior set of shelves then brings other appliances to the fore. A light illuminates the choices.

4 Storing appliances is one thing, and using appliances as storage is another. This dishwasher drawer, located next to the sink, is half the size of a standard dishwasher. Install two of these pint-size appliances and you can unload clean dishes right to the table while dirty dishes get loaded into the other for washing. This system saves steps and eliminates the need for a cabinet for everyday dishes.

5 A small beverage refrigerator allows you to store plenty of drinks without cutting into perishable food storage space.

6 Oddly shaped cabinet spaces often go to waste. These slide-out plastic bins mimic cabinet contours and make use of every cubic inch available.

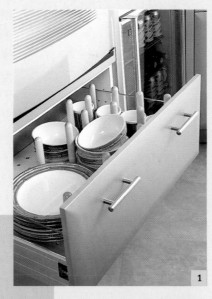

1

2

3

4

5

6

New products and solutions provide more storage options than ever before. Many of these innovations, originally developed for high-end commercial and custom kitchens, are available as off-the-shelf options for kitchens everywhere. This kitchen integrates some of the best ideas around, finding storage in some of the least likely places.

1 Keep perishable foods fresher longer with refrigerator drawers programmed to maintain the precise temperature required for optimum storage of their contents.

2 Lighted, glass-fronted, glass-shelf cabinets offer a great way to store glassware and other items worthy of display. Such cabinets not only add depth and sparkle to a kitchen, they also make it easier to find what you're looking for.

3 Countertop appliance garages are great for reducing visual clutter, but they also reduce counter space. This toaster glides into the cabinet, leaving the countertop unobstructed.

4 A sliding tray—essentially a drawer within a drawer—allows this drawer to hold twice the usual load.

1

Traditional Yet
Modern

This 1920s Mediterranean-style house in Berkeley, California, received a kitchen update that modernizes its classic lines and natural materials with contemporary style. The result is a light, livable, welcoming space for two cooks to work, entertain, and relax with family.

It all started with a complete overhaul of the floor plan, which included relocating the kitchen from the front of the house to the back. There, a modest bump-out expanded the combined kitchen and family room, increasing space, light, and garden views.

The new design is at once bold and contemporary, yet warm and inviting, thanks to a deliberate use of contemporary color and lots of nat-ural materials. Contrasting colors break what has become a rather large room into two more intimately scaled areas—one for food preparation, one for cooking. The result: an artful study in abstract geometry, a hardworking two-cook kitchen, and an inviting gathering space for family and guests.

1 *A mix of materials, colors, and textures—quartersawn ash cabinets, granite countertops, stainless-steel appliances and accents, and a slate wall—combine to create a kitchen that's both interesting and efficient. Frameless windows punctuate the outside wall, admitting light while concealing views of the neighbor's carport. Backless mahogany cabinets (stained red) let the slate wall show through the glass doors. Stainless-steel legs accent each corner of the island, a pleasing contrast to the custom-designed ash-and-steel chairs.*

2 *A floor-to-ceiling desk niche is finished with the same slate used for backsplash walls. It provides a convenient spot to pay bills or catch up on correspondence.*

3 *A trapezoidal wall of slate slides into the dining area. Not just something pretty to look at, it helps define the interface between the dining area and kitchen, as does a change in the direction of the wood-flooring planks.*

4 *The floor plan was completely reworked, moving the kitchen to the back of the house; the former kitchen space was turned into a laundry/powder room area. Two sinks, two dishwashers, a 48-inch commercial range, and a wall oven make food preparation easy for two cooks in the new space.*

2

3

4

FAMILY

DINING

KITCHEN

Before

FAMILY/
BREAKFAST

KITCHEN

LAUNDRY

After

Tavern Transformed

This 1916 tavern-turned-home in an old neighborhood in Chicago has gone through some drastic changes over the years. When it first made the conversion, it received an all-white, Euro-style kitchen, a contemporary look that didn't mesh with the structure's pressed-tin ceilings and other vintage details. But everything deserves a second chance, and today's newly remodeled kitchen features the warmth and durability of traditional materials and the equipment and layout fit for a chef: cookbook author, restaurateur, PBS series host, and food entrepreneur Rick Bayless.

A large central island with a commercial dual-fuel range divides the room into prep and cleanup areas and stores everything needed for either task within a couple steps of one another. Tall ceilings and generous crown moldings on the upper cabinets provide a great venue for displaying collectibles, such as Bayless's collection of handmade Mexican pottery. Uplighting mounted on the cabinet tops bathes the room in indirect light and accents the shape and sparkle of the pots and vases.

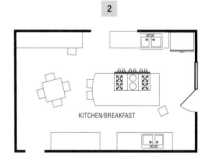

KITCHEN/BREAKFAST

After

1 Natural pine cabinetry with wrought-iron hardware creates an air of warmth and informality. Crown moldings add just a touch of dressy detail, while painted tiles from Mexico and a hand-loomed rug brighten the room with splashes of color.

2 Centered between soapstone sinks on opposite walls, a 9×4-foot island divides the room into prep and cleanup areas and separates the eating area from the work core. The island is topped with butcher block and equipped with a stainless-steel range. A patio door leads to a deck with a container garden.

3 In the built-in hutch, upper glass-fronted cabinets hold glassware, while open shelves house a cookbook collection. A desk keeps a laptop and associated clutter off the 1930s oak table. Linens are stored in lower cabinets.

4 Plants that require minimal light flourish in the north-facing greenhouse windows.

Soapstone for Sinks & *Counters*

It doesn't have the gloss of marble or the glitter of granite, but soft and mottled soapstone—traditionally used for hardworking farmhouse sinks—is a popular countertop material. Its matte finish, velvety feel, and subdued coloration make it the perfect complement to this kitchen's hardworking butcher-block top island and stainless-steel range. Like other stones, soapstone can't be damaged by hot pots and pans, and it doesn't succumb to stains as readily as porous and lighter-color limestone and marble. Although its soft and soapy feel means it scratches and gouges more easily than harder stones such as granite, many believe the minor surface imperfections and wear marks add to its appeal.

131

East by Southwest

What do you do if you want your new kitchen to reflect your heritage, but your roots are divergent, for instance on opposite sides of the country? In this Chicago kitchen, one design style leads and looks for opportunities to bring in the other. More specifically, Williamsburglike colonial style is peppered with Southwestern touches that blend the owners' allegiances to Maryland and Arizona.

The resulting kitchen is anchored on both ends by a brick hearth—a cooking cove at the range on one end and a fireplace in the breakfast area on the other. Between them stands a massive island, which is actually a few pieces of furniture pulled together and fitted with plumbing. To keep with the dark woods typical of colonial style, all the pieces are stained a coffee hue. The kitchen's walls are whitewashed or covered in putty-color tiles, a hue that belongs to both colonial and Southwestern palettes.

To one side of the kitchen, huge hutches flank an apron sink. The sheer turquoise stain of one hutch nods to both colonial and Southwestern styles; the unfinished beamed ceiling leans more toward the south than the northeast. Iron pot racks hung from the ceiling are a colonial touch. On the white oak floor in the breakfast room, a painted rug featuring a Greek-key-and-checkerboard design is pure colonial, but the colors—turquoise, deep red, off-white, and green—emit desert style. The paint was sanded before topping it with varnish to keep it from looking too crisp.

Continued on page 134

1

2

3

4

1 A weathered copper-and-brass faucet at the island's prep sink adds a timeless, character-rich touch.

2 Mission-style furnishings and Southwestern flair go hand in hand. The simplicity of the table and chairs blends well with the dominant colonial theme and the chandelier above.

3 Despite the kitchen's age-old look, this space cooks at modern-day speed thanks to thoughtful planning and cutting-edge appliances.

4 As elegant and spacious as it is, this rectangular kitchen is essentially a fat galley kitchen with an island in between. Its straight path separates at the far end, with an office on one side and a butler's pantry that leads to the formal dining space on the other.

1

2 3

1 The butler's pantry is visible from both the rustic kitchen and the formal dining room. Its elements tend toward the elegant side, providing a graceful transition between the two spaces. Bubbled-glass panes in the upper cabinets recall old-style glass.

2 In the butler's pantry, a Southwestern pinecone motif beautifies the matte-finish tiles.

3 A furniturelike desk slips into this run of cabinets, sporting a natural-finish wood top.

4 The sleek look of this industrial range works nicely surrounded by the brick cove and coffee-hue cabinets. The range hood is hidden in chimneylike brickwork.

5 A painted rug never bunches. In this kitchen, a traditional colonial pattern is rendered on the floor in a Southwestern palette. By sanding the paint before varnishing, a sheer, worn look is achieved. The effect is a subtle complement to the largely unadorned kitchen.

4

5

135

If you're thinking about remodeling an existing kitchen or building a new one, it's a perfect time to evaluate the rooms and areas that surround the traditional kitchen work core. If your kitchen serves as your home's most-used entry, the addition or reworking of a mudroom—perhaps one that accommodates a laundry—could help ease kitchen mess and congestion. Is the problem a lack

See page 141

of storage? Before you tear out a bank of windows to install floor-to-ceiling cabinets, consider whether a separate pantry might make more sense. Are you sick of sweeping the kitchen table free of bills and papers before every meal, or do you need a place for the kids to use the computer while you monitor their Internet surfing? A kitchen office might be just what you need. Finally, if you have a great backyard, deck, or patio and love to entertain outdoors, perhaps a separate outdoor kitchen warrants a place in your plans. In any case, the ideas contained within this chapter are sure to spark some interest.

Rooms
Around the Kitchen

Breakfast Is Served

A place to enjoy breakfast is an integral part of every kitchen. There are as many ways to create a place to eat this meal as there are ways to cook an egg. Here are three diverse examples to consider for your own breakfast nook.

On a Full-Size Table

If you're working with a shallow niche, similar to the one shown *above*, and shelves of collectibles you'd like to display, a banquette simply won't work. As an alternative, this glass-top table visually expands the space and doesn't upstage the handcrafted teapots. The stainless-steel chairs fade into the background too, largely because they're made of the same material as the display shelves. The table centers in the alcove, leaving ample room on one side for a traffic lane.

In the Morning Sun

For an especially sunny and warm place to have breakfast, seek out an east-facing exterior wall or create one. The nook *above*, located off of a kitchen, was made by annexing a few feet of deck space and a very small entryway. Craftsman-style windows, a pewlike L-shape banquette and matching table, and two antique chairs complete the niche.

1 When locating a dining table close to a wall, bear in mind that an adult needs 32 to 36 inches from table to wall to rise or sit down. For room to walk from guest to guest while serving, add another 8 inches.

2 With banquettes, allow 12 inches from the top of the benches to the table surface. If the table overlaps the benches by 3 or 4 inches on each side, average-size adults will be able to use the backrest and still reach their plates.

3 Banquettes are put to good use in a kitchen corner. The craftsman-style units are topped with cushions and pillows. Wainscoting serves as seat backs on one side, and shallow shelving above becomes display space. Good banquette seats are 18 inches high and have a "heel kick" at floor level.

In a Cozy Corner

Because chairs need to slide in and out, and because tables should measure 30 inches across to ensure diners have enough room, a table and chair set isn't the most efficient way to configure an informal eating area. If space is at a premium, consider a banquette instead, as shown *right*. It occupies less than half the floor space that a table and chairs require, yet seats the same number of people.

Kitchen Command Centers

1

2

Do you lack a convenient place in your kitchen to drop the mail, pay bills, check your e-mail, peruse your cookbooks and recipes, or help your kids with homework? These days, more and more kitchens function as planning centers, home offices, homework central, and the place where mail gets opened and routine household business is taken care of. If your kitchen lacks a dedicated space for these activities, you may find that your kitchen table picks up the slack, requiring a clean-up, clear-off operation before each meal. The solution may well be a kitchen command center equipped to handle all these tasks and more. The following suggest a variety of ways to integrate these functions into your kitchen without taking over your dining space or intruding on the cooking work core.

Location, Location, Location

Where you put a kitchen office depends on its size, how many people will use it, and what sort of work will be done there. **Do you need only a desk and a telephone?** Locate your office on the perimeter of the kitchen, away from the main work triangle. This allows the cook to work without bumping into whomever may be working at the desk. For a telephone-answering and bill-paying center, select a 36-inch-wide desk that's about 28 inches tall and has a couple of drawers. Thirty-six inches is wide enough to spread out papers, and the drawers can hold all the necessities for taking messages and paying bills.

Do you need extra storage space? Make room for cubbyholes or deep drawers, which provide convenient spots to stash the kids' schoolbooks and backpacks, especially if they don't have desks in their bedrooms. If your kids will be using the space too, an adjustable-height chair is a wise investment.

Do you need a computer? You can plunk down a laptop anywhere, but a full-size machine requires 5 to 6 linear feet of counter space to fit a printer, keyboard, and a telephone. Ideally, the computer should inhabit a wall opposite the cooking and meal-preparation areas—perhaps separated from those areas by an island or peninsula—both to keep the office clean and to avoid intruding on the cooking core. Allow for plenty of legroom, which also must accommodate your computer's central processing unit. Install a grommet big enough to hold all the wires for the computer, a telephone, lamp, and other appliances and peripherals in the countertop, and channel them to the outlet below.

3

1 *Having a kitchen office doesn't necessarily mean squeezing all parts into a corner. A half-wall separates this kitchen-side office from the work core. The arrangement works well when kids need to use the computer for homework or browsing the Internet: Mom and Dad are able to supervise, even while making dinner. Similarly, one adult can complete a work project or make travel plans while the other scrubs a dirty pot, all while consulting each other easily.*

2 *At the other end of the spectrum is this smidgen of tabletop built into a wall of shelves and cubbies. A laptop's diminutive size makes it all possible because you can tuck it into a drawer when it's not in use, freeing up the desktop for other tasks. Deep built-in shelves hold the printer, books, stereo speakers, and knick knacks. One cubby has a pullout shelf for a TV. Corkboard lets the whole family tack up notes and messages.*

3 *This computer work center, resting between the cooking and eating areas, is slightly removed from main traffic patterns. Raised-panel detailing on the door fronts helps blend the look of the desk right into the woodwork of the 1930s home; a specially designed cabinet in the kneehole area holds the computer's central processing unit.*

Perfect Pantries

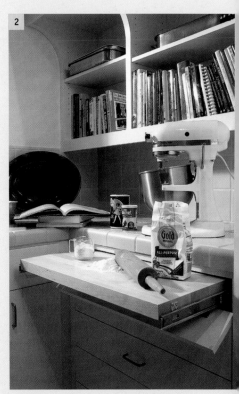

No longer dark, stuffy, little rooms that hide nonperishables, pantries have become practical—not to mention attractive—kitchen storage and work spaces. Accouterments include everything from refrigerators to gardening stations, depending upon the owner's needs. Pantries are even a fine spot to hide a second dishwasher. If your idea of a pantry is just a closet crammed with cans and boxes, check out these eye-opening examples.

Pantry *by Numbers*

Seven: That's the maximum height, in feet, that pantry shelves should rise from the floor because it's the maximum height most people can safely reach with a step stool. Use the top shelves for seldom-used serving pieces and seasonal items.

Twelve: This is the maximum depth, in inches, pantry shelving should delve to prevent "burying" items behind other items, making them hard to reach. For deeper storage, use drawers, cabinets with sliding trays, or swing-out pantry shelves.

1 This pantry's inviting curves make up a friendly-yet-functional shape. A stainless-steel ladder runs along a track that follows the shelves' contour, allowing easy access to even the upper deck in this 10-foot-tall space. Shorter shelves hold baking pans and trays; cubbyholes conceal bottles of wine. An extra refrigerator/freezer gives the room the means to store perishables or garden produce in addition to dry and canned goods.

2 A baking center outfitted with a pullout work board, mixer, and cookbooks makes it possible to do some food prep on-site so there's no need to carry bulk ingredients into a separate room.

3 Specially designed as a place for caterers to prepare, serve, and clean up from parties, this pantry includes a refrigerator, freezer, open storage, a broom closet, a rolling cart that can be taken to other rooms, and storage for small appliances such as food processors, grinders, and fryers.

4 This pantry's generous shelving makes room for buying in bulk—saving you money, trips to the store, and the aggravation of running out of sugar midway through a baking project. A window provides natural light and ventilation. A sink and dishwasher speed cleanup.

The Ideal Pantry is . . .

Convenient: Located in or near the kitchen.

Dry: Many types of food, such as sugar, flour, pasta, crackers, and other loose, dry items, are adversely affected by high humidity.

Cool: Many foods deteriorate faster in warmer environments. Locate cabinets or shelving for food storage on cool outside walls and, if possible, near shaded north-facing windows. Avoid placing pantries near sources of heat such as ranges, ovens, refrigerators, and radiators.

Dark: If you store foods in glass containers, keep your pantry dark. Many foods are light sensitive. Turn off the light when the room is not in use. If the pantry has a window, draw a room-darkening curtain.

The Great Outdoors

Outdoor cooking areas are valuable home improvements from which homeowners can host family cookouts on the grill and full-scale dinner parties with dozens of guests.

Simple outdoor kitchens are comprised of a grill plus a small sink, refrigerator, and storage cabinet. More elaborate outdoor spaces include larger sinks and refrigerators, more storage space for food items, dishes, and serving ware—and, for those who go all out, a dishwasher. In general, the farther the outdoor kitchen is located from the home's main kitchen, the more complete the setup needs to be.

You can customize specialty kitchens with features that support a particular kind of cooking or entertaining simply by incorporating amenities such as wood-fired pizza ovens, wet bars, and fire pits with rotisseries. Design cooking and dining areas to take advantage of existing outdoor structures, or build arbors, pergolas, walls, patios, and decks to complete outdoor rooms that provide both shelter and seating.

Your Outdoor *Kitchen*

To streamline serving and cleanup, situate your outdoor kitchen near your indoor kitchen. If you desire a full-scale setup, complete with a built-in grill, sink, refrigerator, and storage, first analyze where people naturally congregate in your backyard.

To plan the kitchen's size and layout, consider how many people you'll serve and how you entertain. A freestanding dining set may work well for your family, but for large parties you'll need more space for people to stand, walk, serve themselves, and sit.

Incorporate low-maintenance materials, such as brick, cedar, redwood, or teak. Use exterior-grade glazed tiles on both countertops and patio floors—these tiles won't absorb moisture and are easy to clean.

Plan for protection from sun and rain; use existing landscape features or add awnings, latticework, or a louvered roof.

3

4

1 *The craftsman-style architecture of this San Diego home influenced the design of its outdoor kitchen. Twin pergolas provide shade and a sense of enclosure; the structure's vigorous Climbing Cecile Bruner roses will make a shady respite in a year or two, even on the sunniest of days.*

2 *A brick wall paired with a dense hedge gives this outdoor kitchen plenty of privacy. The wall also serves as a backsplash for the granite countertop with a built-in stainless-steel grill. Wood doors with rustic, black-iron strap hinges open to storage below.*

3 *A massive river-rock fireplace acts as a kitchen focal point. Its raised, extra-wide hearth doubles as casual seating for both children and adults.*

4 *A generous-size table and plenty of seating—made of attractive, low-maintenance, all-weather teak—provide a great setting for an outdoor meal.*

Mudrooms and Laundries

[1] This 8×15-foot gardener's mudroom serves as a transitional space from a back deck into the kitchen. It incorporates a potting bench with a big sink that's also useful for scrubbing roasting pans and other large cookware.

[2] Boots, umbrellas, raincoats, and other soggy stuff store in a closet with a floor drain. The closet's louvered door allows air to circulate.

[3] An easy-to-mop tile floor and two floor mats—one outside the door and one inside—keep dirt from migrating into the main house. Shaker pegs are perfect for hanging dry clothing and accessories; a bench provides a great place to toss backpacks or change footgear.

[4] Located between the kitchen and the entry from the driveway and garage, this 10×15-foot utility room features abundant storage in white-laminate cabinetry that wipes clean in a jiffy. One cabinet catches laundry sent down a chute from upstairs. The room's opposite wall hosts a washer, dryer, and treatment sink.

[5] A spacious janitor's sink works perfectly for bathing small pets; it's also a great place to rinse muddy shoes and drain wet boots.

The "cleanup zone" conjures images of sinks, dishwashers, garbage disposals, and perhaps trash compactors. If the scope is widened to rooms around the kitchen, two additional areas might come to mind: mudrooms and laundries. The former keeps the worst of the great outdoors from penetrating your home's living areas, and the latter is the hub of clothes washing, drying, and ironing. Often, both functions are integrated into the same space.

If you're considering a kitchen redesign, it's a good time to think about integrating a laundry and mudroom into your plans. A laundry room or mudroom doesn't have to take up much space: 20 square feet is enough. For many families, especially those with children, pets, or a love of outdoor activities such as sports or gardening, a mudroom with the washer or dryer nearby is ideal. If there's room, you can accommodate a specialty area, be it for potting plants, sewing, gift wrapping, or pet grooming.

Continued on page 148

Mudroom *Manifesto*

Mudrooms come in many shapes and sizes, so finding a place to worm one into your home may be easier than you think, especially if you keep these concepts in mind:

Start by the door. Your quest for a mudroom begins near an entryway. It's almost effortless to drop gear by the door and pick it up again when leaving, so it makes sense to position mudrooms in proximity to entries. Doing so also confines dirty shoes and gear to one easy-to-clean area.

Try small spaces. Even tight areas, such as large closets, wide hallways, and ample foyers, make fine candidates for mudroom-type storage. A few hooks or a bench is helpful. Devoting a single wall to shelving, cubbies, cabinets, or locker-style compartments enhances storage and organization.

Check the porch's potential. Porches and sunrooms on the backs of older homes qualify as good candidates for conversion to mudrooms because they're near the yard and garage.

4

3

5

In order for your mudroom or laundry to serve your needs, you'll have to equip it properly. Sinks, cabinets, countertops, foldout ironing centers, and new, quieter appliances make it easier and more convenient to perform tasks—and keep the room neat and organized at the same time.

2

3

Laundry List Consider the following when designing a laundry room:

Slip in a sink. Even a small sink can be used to soak grimy clothes. If you have the room, opt for a deep bowl, which doubles as a place to rinse off garden tools or a bathtub for the family pet.

Install base cabinets. They not only hide the sink plumbing, they also conceal detergent bottles and other laundry necessities. If you have room for an additional cabinet or two, consider storing a slide-in hamper and a pullout wastebasket. Open shelves, or more cabinets, provide places to stash cleaning supplies, rags, and other necessities.

Handle the load. A few linear feet of laminate countertop—or a small table—provides a handy spot for sorting dirty clothes, as well as a convenient area to pile clothes straight out of the dryer. To hang shirts or jeans to drip-dry, include a rod or several inexpensive metal pegs over the sink, or design a special open closet with a floor drain.

Disguise your ironing zone. Hide built-in, foldout ironing boards in a tall, wall-mount cabinet. Mount a shelf for the iron in there too, along with an electrical outlet. With such a setup, you're ready to press clothes in a jiffy—without lugging out the ironing board and plugging in the iron every time.

Explore appliance options. Today's washers and dryers make less noise and are more efficient than older models. Horizontal-axis machines use less water and energy, and are harder on dirt and easier on clothing than standard machines. Some models are made small enough to slide under a countertop, freeing up even more floor space. Stackable models feature full-size performance but take up half the space of freestanding units.

1 _Raising standard base cabinets 3 inches elevates the countertop in this laundry room for greater comfort when standing and folding clothes. The rubber flooring eases back strain. Baskets for sorting clothes slide into open niches, and a curtain rod between the wall cabinets serves as a clothesline for the south-facing window._

2 _This full-service mudroom also includes a sewing center. After washing and drying, laundry gets pressed on full-size and sleeve-size ironing boards that drop out of a vertical cabinet. The cabinet also accommodates the iron and an electrical outlet. Pressed clothes hang on the pullout rods to the right._

3 _Elsewhere in the same room, a customized bin organizes paper, ribbons, boxes, and other gift-wrapping gear in one convenient spot._

4 _Across the way, a pullout shelf accommodates a sewing machine; open shelves above store threads, needles, and fabric swatches. Slide the shelf in to conceal the whole area behind a cabinet door, keeping the countertop clear._

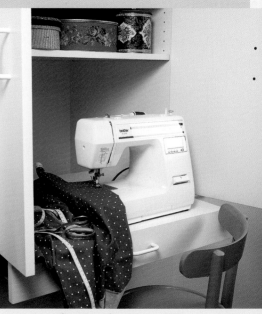

4

Continued on page 150

Laundries aren't just for washing clothes—they're also ideal places for indulging in a favorite hobby or craft. Clad in rich blue laminate, this laundry room doubles as a sewing room for an avid quilter. It features laundry facilities, a sink, two sewing machines, and a refrigerator for beverages.

1 This simple, spacious layout offers separate areas for laundry, cleanup, and sewing.

2 Counters placed at two different heights are clad in stainless steel, which resists scratching from scissors and pins. The V-shape countertop gives extra depth for sewn material and allows space on either side for a level feed into the machines. Upper cabinets extend fabric storage to the ceiling.

3 Lower cabinets conveniently stash dirty laundry. Colored items go in a blue basket, whites in a white basket.

4 This ironing cabinet includes a shelf with a cutout that makes room for the ironing board without sacrificing shelf space.

The recipe for a great kitchen of any size or style includes a mix of just the right ingredients. In this chapter, you'll find a review of appliances, cabinetry, countertops, sinks and faucets, flooring, and light fixtures—the staple elements from which every kitchen is composed. The word of the day is variety: There are more products, more types and styles with more features and functions available than ever before. Some items, such as synthetic stone countertops and laminate flooring, resemble hard-to-find—or hard-to-afford—premium natural materials. Other items, such as combination ovens, integrate the best of several technologies (in this case, microwave, convection, and thermal ovens) in one high-performance product. Still other products are being rediscovered (linoleum), or are newly improved, earth-friendly, or superior in looks or performance. This chapter prepares you for what you'll find when you visit home improvement centers and specialty shops, or when you first talk with an architect, a designer, or a contractor.

See page 158

Kitchen Elements

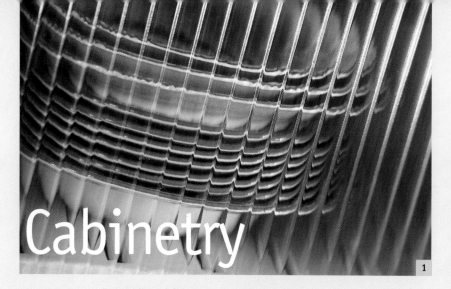

Cabinetry

Cabinets often consume 40 percent of a new or completely remodeled kitchen's budget, so select yours carefully to ensure you get what you want. Fortunately, manufactured cabinets have improved quality and offer an impressive list of standard features and furniturelike style formerly available to custom buyers. Features that you can order with many stock and semi-custom cabinets include recycling bin inserts, drawer dividers, angled spice inserts, bread savers, pasta bins, wine racks, appliance garages, file drawers, and lazy Susans. Furniturelike details include fretwork, carved onlays, arched valances, punched-tin door inserts, clear and decorative glass doors, and footed base cabinets. Turned legs make kitchen cabinetry that's reminiscent of fine period furniture, a detail that's especially attractive in homes that have open floor plans where the kitchen work core is on display to living and dining areas.

While you're selecting features and style, keep your eye out for quality. A little experience with cabinetry anatomy will help you buy wisely.

Types

Choose face-frame or frameless.
Face-frame cabinets attach framing to the front of the cabinet box. This type of construction is sturdy and stable and results in a more traditional look. Drawers and pullouts are somewhat smaller than the overall cabinet dimensions, because they must fit within the framing. As a result, these cabinets offer less capacity than their frameless counterparts. The grain on good-quality face-frame cabinets matches that of the drawers.

Frameless cabinets have door hinges that attach to the inside of the cabinet for a contemporary look. They have a somewhat larger capacity than framed cabinets, but are more difficult to plan for and install, because you must take into account door clearances and filler panels, which are needed when cabinets are installed at an angle to one another.

Materials

Three materials form the guts of most cabinets.

Particleboard serves as the base for most laminate and some veneered cabinets. Look for 45-pound commercial grade particleboard; poorer grades won't hold screws well.

Medium-density fiberboard (MDF) is a high-quality substrate material that offers a smooth surface and edges that you can shape and paint.

Plywood is the strongest of the materials and offers the best structural support.

Joints

Joints give cabinets their strength and stability; the better the joint, the better the cabinet.

Butt joints are the least sturdy option: The cabinet pieces are simply glued to each other.

Dado joints are more robust than butt joints. The sides fit into grooves cut into the cabinet back and the face frame.

Gussets are triangular braces glued

into the upper corners of the cabinet boxes to add even more strength.

Drawers

Look for quality drawers that:

Glide smoothly on ball-bearing-equipped nylon wheels that roll on 75-pound capacity metal rails.

Extend fully so you have full access to the contents without removing the drawer from the cabinet.

Don't wobble when fully extended.

Close automatically if pulled out less than 1 inch on self-closing guides.

Have dovetail or dowel joints at the corners for long-term durability.

Are sturdily made of ½- or ¾-inch solid wood sides and plywood bottom panels that are set into grooves.

Cabinet Fronts

Choose from the following three kinds:

Full-inset fronts are flush with the cabinet frame. Because these require excellent craftsmanship, only custom cabinets feature them.

Partial-overlay fronts conceal the opening but reveal some of the frame. This style is affordable because it's easier to construct.

Full-overlay doors are the only option available for frameless cabinetry because they cover the entire box front. When used on face-frame cabinetry, a full overlay covers the entire frame.

Doors

Most cabinet doors feature versatile frame-and-panel construction; custom cabinets often feature solid wood.

Frame-and-panel doors "float" a panel of solid wood, veneered panel, or clear or patterned glass within the wood frame.

Solid-wood doors consist of several pieces of wood glued together for the appearance of one solid panel. For stability, manufacturers screw wood crosspieces to the back.

Shelves and Trays

The following three options help you organize cabinet space.

Shelves are best constructed from ¾-inch, 45-pound commercial-grade particleboard covered with a durable material, such as laminate or melamine.

Adjustable shelves are held in place with removable metal pins or plastic clips inserted into holes.

Roll-out trays make better use of space than shallow shelves, and the low sides provide easy access. Often subjected to heavier weight than drawers, roll-out trays require the same high-quality glides.

3

1 See-through cabinet fronts allow partial visibility, so locating items is easier. Here, reeded glass creates an abstract pattern.

2 This slide-out drawer houses bins that organize recyclables. Like many other special features, it was once only available to custom buyers, but is now a popular option for those in the market for stock cabinets.

3 Roll-out trays are replacing fixed shelves in many kitchens because they offer easier access. Sturdy metal glide rails make it possible for trays to accommodate heavy loads without wobbling.

1

Countertops

Countertops rank up there with the most important features of any kitchen. A dizzying array of materials makes for innumerable options, from standard laminate to contemporary concrete and everything in between. Choose just one of these materials for your kitchen or use two or more to customize work areas and attractively break up long surfaces. You might, for example, set a stone slab in the baking area for rolling dough and a different material on the perimeter cabinetry. Generally stone, faux-stone, concrete, and stainless steel prove most expensive; laminate is generally the least expensive. Cost varies widely, however, depending upon region, pattern, and installation, so check with a home center or local fabricator to get a realistic estimate.

Ceramic tile handles hot pans without scorching, is moisture-resistant, and comes in a host of colors, patterns, and textures, making the decorative possibilities infinite—think geometric designs, borders, and mosaics. The tiles themselves wipe clean with a damp cloth but surrounding grout joints sometimes stain. To minimize discoloration, install a tiled countertop using narrow grout joints, epoxy grout, or perhaps even a darker color grout.

Concrete is an increasingly popular option that complements a variety of kitchen aesthetics. It may be gray or dyed and inlaid with other elements to create custom looks. The material must be sealed regularly and stands up well under heat, but it still is subject to stains. Three techniques are used to install concrete countertops:

First, you can order concrete tiles and concrete slabs from home improvement centers and install them on site. (If desired, you can have them colored before they're installed.) Second, you can have site-poured counters built by a contractor in your home. Forms are built on top of cabinets, then filled with concrete. Some site-poured countertops feature inlaid decorative materials, such as metal or stone. Finally, you can install site-poured counters that require metal forms that remain in place, adding a contrasting gleaming edge to the grainy material. To compare, the price of a concrete counter is somewhat less than stone, but a bit more than butcher block, and about the same as stainless steel.

Engineered quartz has an appearance, composition, weight, and price that are all comparable to granite. Made of quartz that's bound together with space-age polymers, it captures the crystalline sparkle and density of granite, but it is nonporous so it does not require sealing and is less susceptible to stains. Manufacturers claim that it's tougher than granite and less susceptible to chipping and cracking.

Granite is prized for its natural beauty and durability, whether polished to a high gloss or honed to a pleasing matte finish. Its sparkly, variegated, crystalline structure makes for a lively play of light on its surface and has the added bonus of camouflaging errant crumbs. Granite is ultrasmooth and cool, providing a suitable surface for kneading and rolling dough. On the downside, it requires periodic treatment with a nontoxic penetrating sealant to keep its surface in top condition, and a sharp blow with a pointed object can chip it. Solid granite is expensive; for a lower cost option, consider 12×12-inch granite tiles.

Laminate, an affordable, durable,

low-maintenance surface offers a tremendous range of colors, patterns, and textures, some of which look like more expensive, natural materials. While laminate stands up to grease and stains and wipes clean with soap and water, it's vulnerable to sharp knives or hot pans. Heavy blows can dent the surface, and prolonged exposure to water may dissolve glue lines and cause the subsurface to warp. Better grades of laminate feature color throughout the material, making scratches and chips less visible. You can buy laminate countertop sections finished with a variety of front edge treatments, with or without attached backsplashes.

Marble, like granite, has a cool-to-the-touch surface that makes it ideal for baking and candymaking, but it is much softer and more porous than granite. It sometimes fractures along veining; offers less resistance to stains, scratches, and general wear; and must be sealed often.

Soapstone, a traditional choice for old-fashioned scullery sinks, has a muted gray-green color, mellow luster, and velvety feel. Soapstone is stain- and heat-resistant and

durable, but it's also soft, distresses to a patina over years of use, and needs to be sealed.

Solid surfacing, made entirely of plastic resin composites, comes in a variety of thicknesses. A wide range of colors, patterns, and natural-material look-alikes is available. The material is also known for its design flexibility, allowing the creation of special effects through inlays of contrasting colors. Because color runs through the material, nicks are camouflaged. The nonporous material resists stains, but does scratch and scorch. Minor damage sands out.

Stainless steel is popular for creating commercial-style kitchens. It is also the only material besides solid surfacing that allows one-piece countertop/sink formations, eliminating the dirt-catching seam between the counter and the sink bowl. Stainless withstands hot pots and pans and is easy to clean. It does scratch, though, so you can't use it for a cutting surface. Surface finishes range from a mirrorlike gleam to a matte glow; you can also opt for lightly brushed, relief-stamped, or embossed. The shinier the surface, the more noticeable fingerprints and marks will be.

1 Ceramic tile is a perennial favorite for countertops and backsplashes not only because it's durable and easy to clean, but because its color and design possibilities are endless.

2 Gorgeous and nearly indestructible, granite is available in a wide variety of colors and grain patterns. Unlike more porous stones such as marble and limestone, it won't stain.

3 Stainless-steel countertops have made their way from commercial kitchens to high-end residential installations.

159

Sinks and Faucets

1

Most of your kitchen chores involve the sink, so choose a bowl and faucet that are versatile and durable. A wide range of options makes it easy to find something that suits your needs and budget.

Sink Materials
A variety of metals, natural materials, and faux-natural materials is available for sinks.
Stainless steel is the most popular choice: It's durable and lightweight, making it easy to install. Thickness and finish contribute to quality. A thick 19-gauge sink won't dent easily, a nickel-and-stainless composition wards off water spots, and a brushed finish—rather than a mirror finish—conceals scratches. Stainless sinks are among the least expensive sink options, although restaurant-quality, one-piece stainless sink-and-counter combinations that are excep-

tionally durable and easy to clean can be pricey.

Enameled cast-iron sinks not only perform well, they also provide the kitchen with an extra shot of color—especially those that have apron fronts, which expose the front of the sink. Available in black, white, and a rainbow of colors, these sinks are extremely durable. Enameled cast-iron sinks are more expensive than stainless sinks, less forgiving of dropped glassware and china than stainless, and because they're quite heavy, they can be difficult to install.
Vitreous china is easy to clean, colorful, and attractive, but it is also susceptible to chipping.
Quartz composite resists scratches and stains, and the material's wide range of colors and grains looks great with stone countertops.
Solid-surface materials offer many solid color choices as well as stone look-alikes. Like commercial-quality stainless, one-piece, integrated sinks and countertops are available for a seamless look and easy cleaning.
Soapstone sinks are experiencing a comeback as people rediscover the material's muted, green-gray tones, solid feel, and soft patina.
Copper offers a rich color accent, but eventually oxidizes to a gray-green color unless polished regularly. Because copper is soft, these sinks dent easily.

Sink Types
The type you choose largely depends on your countertop material.
Self-rimming sinks, the most commonly used variety, are also the easiest to install. With a rim that overlays the countertop, these sinks easily retrofit into existing countertops (as long as the opening is the same size). They also protect laminate counter-

tops from moisture damage. Although debris collects around the sink's rim, it is pretty simple to clean. **Undermount** sinks mount to the bottom of a stone or solid-surface countertop, emphasizing the countertop material and making cleanup easy, because you can sweep crumbs directly from the counter into the sink without the risk of catching them on the rim. You generally can't use them with laminate countertops, because they expose the counter substrate. Both sink and countertop require expert installation for a precise, clean fit.

Integrated bowl sinks and countertops are made of one seamless material for a flawless look and easy cleanup. Material options are limited to higher-cost stainless and solid-surface products and sometimes to custom designs and special installations.

Sink Configurations and Options

You used to have but one decision to make: one bowl or two. Now you have many more options.

Single-bowl sinks are ideal for soaking big pots and pans.

Double-bowl sinks handle food preparation and dish-soaking simultaneously.

Triple-bowl sinks add a center-well disposer.

L-shape sinks in either double- or triple-bowl configurations are good for corner locations in kitchens with limited counter space.

Extra-deep bowls—some as deep as 14 inches—are useful for filling tall pots and washing large quantities of dishes and cookware.

Fitted cutting boards partially cover one basin, freeing up counter space.

Faucets

While the sink category can be broken down into a few materials and types, the same can't be said for faucets. Brushed and polished chrome are still staples, but they've been joined by faucets of brass, powder-coated epoxy in bright colors, and even gold plate. A wide variety of reproduction and vintage-look styles is available, as is a range of contemporary designs.

Commercial faucets and accessories, such as pot-fillers that rise to fill large containers and high-capacity sprayers that help rinse cookware, are now available for home use. Even conventional residential faucets have become far more versatile, with scraper-spray and brush-spray combinations or pullout wands that

change from stream to spray to fill large pots or rinse dishes. Washerless and ceramic disk valves have replaced leaky rubber washers. Antiscald faucets protect children from hot-water burns and integrated purified water dispensers eliminate the need to buy bottled water.

1 Side-by-side apron-front farmhouse sinks blend well with the pine cabinetry in this country kitchen.

2 Paired with a granite countertop, this brushed stainless-steel undermount sink and complementary vintage-style single-lever faucet create a timeless look. Undermount sinks are great for showing off the full thickness of counters made from natural or engineered stone or solid surfacing.

Flooring

As you prepare and serve meals, pack lunches, and go about other daily tasks, you're on your feet a lot in the kitchen. That's why it's important to choose the best flooring for your needs. Base your selection on a balance of comfort, maintenance, durability, and good looks. Here's a sampling of what's available.

Bamboo is becoming an increasingly popular choice. It is durable, eco-friendly, and looks like hardwood (it's actually three layers of grass laminated under high pressure to create planks). Three coats of acrylic urethane make the surface durable and resistant to water, mildew, and insect damage. Harder than maple and oak, bamboo also expands and contracts less. Because bamboo plants (not the kind eaten by pandas) produce new shoots, it's an easily sustainable product that may be harvested after three and five years of growth. Bamboo flooring comes unfinished or finished, and you can glue or nail it to a subfloor. It is fairly costly.

Ceramic tile comes in a variety of sizes and colors that allow you to create exciting patterns. Tiles are available both glazed and unglazed; a glazed finish is a good choice for kitchens because it prevents moisture from soaking in, although high-traffic areas with glazed tiles may eventually show some wear. Ceramic tile is durable, resistant to moisture, and generally low-maintenance, making it especially suitable for kitchens and surrounding rooms such as mudrooms and laundry rooms. On the downside, ceramic tile often feels cold, is unforgiving when you drop glassware, and can be difficult to stand on for long periods of time. Further, food and dirt collect in the grout lines. The cost for both materials and installation varies widely depending on the type and dimensions of the tile used, the complexity of the design, and the amount of subfloor preparation required.

Cork provides a resilient, cushioned surface that is quiet underfoot, comfortable, and moisture-resistant. Made from renewable bark harvested from cork oak trees in Mediterranean forests, cork requires a urethane finish for easy sweeping and mopping. Cork comes in tiles or planks, which allow for easy repair should damage occur. Installation is similar to vinyl tile. This type of flooring can last for decades when cared for correctly: Every few years you must sand the old finish and reapply new urethane. The cost of cork flooring is moderately high.

Hardwood brings its warmth and classic good looks into a kitchen. It's available in many species; in solid, engineered, or parquet form; and it is sold prefinished or unfinished. Solid planks are most common, and you can sand and refinish them many times if they are stained or damaged, giving them a long life. Engineered planks consist of two or more layers of wood laminated together (a hardwood veneer "wear" layer and lower layers of softwood). Because the wear layer is relatively thin, you can not continually refinish. Generally solid wood floors are site-finished, whereas engineered wood floors are prefinished. In both cases, new clear finishes are tougher, more durable, and water-resistant than ever, although wood may still be susceptible to water damage in high-traffic areas. The cost of hardwood flooring is moderate.

Laminates offer the look of wood, tile, stone, and other natural materials at a comparably lower price. Early-generation laminates required installers to glue planks together, a tedious process that sometimes resulted in failed joints and moisture damage. Laminates now snap together, cutting installation time dramatically and resulting in tighter, more even, watertight joints. Note that some laminate products are not recommended for use in areas exposed to high humidity such as bathrooms or mudrooms, and most

manufacturers recommend mopping up standing water promptly. Available in squares, strips, or rectangles, laminate is durable, easy to clean, and requires little maintenance. Keep in mind that it can't be refinished or restained like wood. The cost is moderate.

Linoleum, which is made of primarily natural materials, is making a comeback. Not to be confused with vinyl, which is made from petroleum-base polyvinyl chloride, linoleum is made of natural linseed oil, resin, cork, limestone, and wood flour mixed with pigments, then rolled onto a jute backing and dried. Soft underfoot, it comes in both tiles and sheets of solid or flecked colors and is easy to care for. As the linseed oil dries, it actually becomes harder and more durable than vinyl. Although old-style linoleum tended to fade over time, today's linoleum offers bright lasting color. Linoleum flooring is moderately high in cost.

Stone is an elegant flooring choice. Harder varieties, notably granite,

require little maintenance and are nearly indestructible. Others, such as marble and limestone, are more porous, stain easily, and require more maintenance. Some varieties, such as slate, crack and chip. Stone tends to be expensive and, like ceramic tiles, is cold, hard, and unforgiving. The cost is high, and professional installation often is required.

Vinyl is a good-looking, low-cost, and easy-care choice. You'll find an enormous selection of colors and styles, including well-designed stone, tile, and hardwood look-alikes. Vinyl is available in sheets and tiles. Some tiles are available in easy-to-install, self-adhesive form, although they tend to eventually loosen and admit moisture and dirt. Less-expensive vinyl may puncture, fade, and discolor quickly, whereas good-quality, higher-cost sheet vinyl looks good, is easy to maintain, and lasts for many years. The cost of vinyl is low, although do-it-yourselfers may find it equally affordable to install laminate, tile, or wood.

3

Bright Ideas

Lighting is a major tool for making your kitchen livable and inviting. When planning a lighting scheme, don't think only of electrical fixtures: Windows that bring in great views and large doses of sunshine are great sources of light. Weigh storage needs with your desire for more natural light, and you may decide to sacrifice a few upper cabinets for more windows. To keep your kitchen light and bright throughout the day and evening, keep the following lighting basics in mind.

General, or ambient, lighting radiates a comfortable level of brightness throughout a room. A room is usually more pleasing when the general lighting comes from a blend of sources. In smaller kitchens (less than 120 square feet), you could center one ceiling-mounted fixture

(use two or more for larger kitchens) and add recessed spotlights to the perimeter. Or, you can use perimeter soffit lights that direct light upward to reflect off the ceiling. As a guideline, provide at least 100 watts of incandescent light or 25 watts of fluorescent light for each 50 square feet of floor space.

Task lighting illuminates a specific area, such as a sink, food preparation area, or cleanup center. Its point is to prevent eyestrain, and you can create it with undercabinet lights as well as ceiling- or wall-mounted fixtures. When formulating a lighting scheme, be sure that workers won't block light-illuminating work surfaces. Generally, you should provide each work center with a minimum of 100 to 150 watts of incandescent light or 25 to 35 watts of fluorescent light. When used for undercabinet lighting, fluorescent tubes should extend along two-thirds of the length of the counter they light and provide about 8 watts of power per lineal foot of counter. For example, a 6-foot run of counter requires a 4-foot fluorescent tube rated at 48 watts.

Accent lighting, a decorative tool, spotlights the best features of your room and draws attention away from stacks of dirty dishes. Track, recessed, or wall-mounted fixtures—often equipped with the focused, bright-white beam of a halogen light—provide useful accent illumination. Designers today make it a point to include beautiful indirect lighting techniques: behind glass-fronted cabinets, over the tops of cabinetry, bouncing off the ceiling, and tucked into cabinet toe-kicks to show off flooring.

Bulbs

The types of lightbulbs available have widened considerably in recent years. Whether you're building or remodeling a kitchen, now is a great time to rethink what's supplying your artificial light and make sure you're getting the most—and the best kind of—light for your money.

Incandescent bulbs are traditionally used for most household illumination. They're inexpensive, but they don't last particularly long. Most of the energy they consume produces heat, not light, making them energy inefficient and adding to the load on your cooling system during warm weather. They're a good choice for lights that are rarely used, because their initial cost is low, and if they're only switched on for a few minutes a day (as in a closet) it might take decades to recoup the initial investment of a higher-priced but more-efficient bulb.

EnergyMiser or Supersaver bulbs are incandescents that use 5 to 13 percent less energy than traditional incandescents with a very minimal reduction in light output. They cost slightly more but easily recoup the difference in energy savings over the course of their lives. These bulbs are great for moderate-use fixtures, or for anyone who has an aversion to fluorescent light but still wants to save some energy.

Halogen bulbs are more efficient than incandescents and last three to four times longer. These are great for track and spotlights, because you can use a lower wattage bulb and get the same illumination you'd get from larger-watt incandescents. Some halogen lights have the added advantage of being small and can produce a very concentrated white light, making them ideal for highly directional accent lighting.

Compact fluorescent lights screw into the same sockets as incandescents, but use about 75 percent less energy than incandescent bulbs and last 10 times longer. Although they cost more—sometimes up to $15 each—they save many times their purchase price in energy over the course of their lives. And, because they last so long, they're an especially great choice for fixtures that are hard to access and, therefore, hard to change. They're available in light outputs that correspond to most typical incandescent bulbs.

Linear fluorescent lights are the familiar fluorescent tubes that have been lighting schools, offices, basements, shops, and kitchens for decades. They're a great choice for illuminating large spaces with even, glare-free, shadow-free illumination.

1 *Pendant lights provide task lighting above islands and countertops. A wide variety of styles and finishes is available. Some hang from tracks, allowing you to change their placement.*

2 *The light fixtures above this island reflect light off the ceiling; the room glows with soft, nondirectional ambient lighting. Halogen spotlights under the range hood provide direct bright white task lighting to the cooktop.*

165

Now that you are familiar with the options available for making your kitchen more efficient and attractive, this chapter offers additional insights to help you launch your dream, as well as an extensive list of resources and contact information to help you turn it into a beautiful reality.

The strategies you will find here will help you begin your kitchen-building or -remodeling adventure on the right foot so your kitchen becomes the best that it can be.

Start by turning the page and completing the kitchen remodeling checklist, which will help you take inventory of what's in your present kitchen and what you want in your new one. Then take a look at the various types of kitchen configurations and work zones you might want to incorporate. After that, consider the various types of professionals who can help you with your project. Before you meet with them, use the Kitchen Planning Kit to sketch out some design ideas, and review the information on selecting a pro to make sure you hire the best help available.

Toward the end of the chapter you'll find information on funding options and some savvy suggestions about how you can control costs. Finally, take a good look at the comprehensive resources section, which lists contact information for professional associations, books, magazines, websites, and product manufacturers.

Strategies
& Resources

Kitchen Wish List

Planning the kitchen you want requires that you understand the kitchen you have. Then you need to think about what you'd like to change and how you'd change it.

This checklist will help you identify what kind of kitchen you're living with now, what its advantages and drawbacks are, what your needs are, and what you'd like to have in your new kitchen.

First, evaluate the kitchen you have now using the checklist at right. Use the priority box in the far-right column to indicate how important it is to rectify any problems you identify. Use the following number system, or devise your own: 1 = must fix, 2 = want to fix, 3 = would be nice to fix, but can live with it the way it is.

Consider how the higher-priority problems may be rectified in a renovation, or avoided altogether if you're building a new kitchen.

Then work your way through the checklist on the opposite page. Note how you use your current kitchen, and how you'd like to use your new or remodeled one. You may wish to prioritize kitchen functions using the following number system: 1 = must have, 2 = want to have, 3 = would be nice to have, but can do without.

With your prioritized kitchen uses in mind, continue through the questionnaire, noting what storage needs, work centers, and appliances your new or remodeled kitchen will have.

Refer to this checklist as you continue to plan your kitchen, and take it with you when you talk to your kitchen designer, architect, or contractor.

Kitchen Evaluation

Use this list of questions to identify the features of your current kitchen that you want to change when you build or remodel.

Priority (1, 2, 3)

Traffic

- Do entries impede the work core? _____
- Does the table block entries? _____
- Does traffic interrupt cooking? _____
- Are other traffic problems apparent? _____

Cooking

- When preparing meals, are you cut off from others? _____
- Are there workstations for multiple cooks? _____
- Are there too many steps between appliances and the sink? _____
- Is there ample counter space beside the cooktop and refrigerator? _____
- Does your kitchen meet the needs of your special cooking interests? _____

Cleanup

- Is the dishwasher near the sink? _____
- Should the table be closer to the sink and dishwasher? _____
- Could you benefit from a second dishwasher? _____
- Is there a place for recyclables? _____

Storage

- Are your cabinets crowded? _____
- Could you relocate a passageway and reclaim space for cabinetry? _____
- Would you like a walk-in pantry or a pantry cabinet? _____
- Are your existing refrigerator and freezer large enough? _____

Surfaces

- Are you pleased with the current surfaces? _____
- Are the surfaces easy to clean? _____
- Is the flooring comfortable? _____

Light and Views

- Is your kitchen shadowy? _____
- Do you have pleasant views from the sink and the range? _____

Dining

- Do you have a place for dining in the kitchen? _____
- Do you encounter seating difficulties when you entertain? _____

Checklist

Use this list to determine how you use your kitchen, how you'd like to use your kitchen, and what appliances you have or need.

Kitchen Uses	Current Kitchen	New Kitchen	Priority (1, 2, 3)
• Computing	☐	☐	_____
• Entertaining	☐	☐	_____
• Family cooking	☐	☐	_____
• Gourmet cooking	☐	☐	_____
• Homework	☐	☐	_____
• Laundry	☐	☐	_____
• TV viewing	☐	☐	_____

Storage	Current Kitchen	New Kitchen	Priority (1, 2, 3)
• Cleaning products	☐	☐	_____
• Food	☐	☐	_____
• Linens	☐	☐	_____
• Separate butler's pantry	☐	☐	_____
• Shelves	☐	☐	_____
• Small appliances	☐	☐	_____
• Specialty dish	☐	☐	_____
• Standard dish	☐	☐	_____
• Utensils	☐	☐	_____

Work Centers	Current Kitchen	New Kitchen	Priority (1, 2, 3)
• Cleanup	☐	☐	_____
• Cooking	☐	☐	_____
• Food prep	☐	☐	_____
• Food storage	☐	☐	_____
• Formal dining	☐	☐	_____
• Informal dining	☐	☐	_____
• Planning	☐	☐	_____
• Specialty	☐	☐	_____

Small Appliances	Current Kitchen	New Kitchen	Priority (1, 2, 3)
• Baby food maker	☐	☐	_____
• Blender	☐	☐	_____
• Bread machine	☐	☐	_____
• Cappuccino maker	☐	☐	_____
• Coffeemaker	☐	☐	_____
• Deep fat fryer	☐	☐	_____
• Electric can opener	☐	☐	_____
• Electric crockery cooker	☐	☐	_____
• Electric dehydrator	☐	☐	_____
• Electric juicer	☐	☐	_____
• Electric grill	☐	☐	_____
• Electric knife sharpener	☐	☐	_____

Small Appliances	Current Kitchen	New Kitchen	Priority (1, 2, 3)
• Electric wok	☐	☐	_____
• Espresso maker	☐	☐	_____
• Flour/grain mill	☐	☐	_____
• Food processor	☐	☐	_____
• Ice cream maker	☐	☐	_____
• Meat grinder	☐	☐	_____
• Mixer, hand	☐	☐	_____
• Mixer, stand	☐	☐	_____
• Pasta machine	☐	☐	_____
• Popcorn popper	☐	☐	_____
• Rice cooker	☐	☐	_____
• Toaster	☐	☐	_____
• Toaster oven	☐	☐	_____
• Yogurt maker	☐	☐	_____

Large Appliances	Current Kitchen	New Kitchen	Priority (1, 2, 3)
• Cooktop	☐	☐	_____
• Dishwasher	☐	☐	_____
• Dishwasher, second	☐	☐	_____
• Disposal	☐	☐	_____
• Freezer	☐	☐	_____
• Oven, combination	☐	☐	_____
• Oven, convection	☐	☐	_____
• Oven, conventional	☐	☐	_____
• Oven, dual-fuel	☐	☐	_____
• Oven, microwave	☐	☐	_____
• Oven, microwave (second)	☐	☐	_____
• Range, freestanding	☐	☐	_____
• Refrigerator	☐	☐	_____
• Refrigerator drawers	☐	☐	_____
• Sink, single-bowl	☐	☐	_____
• Sink, double-bowl	☐	☐	_____
• Sink, triple-bowl	☐	☐	_____
• Sink, secondary prep	☐	☐	_____
• Trash compactor	☐	☐	_____
• Vent, downdraft	☐	☐	_____
• Vent, overhead	☐	☐	_____
• Warming drawers	☐	☐	_____
• Washer/dryer	☐	☐	_____
• Water purifier	☐	☐	_____
• Wine cooler	☐	☐	_____

Kitchen Configurations

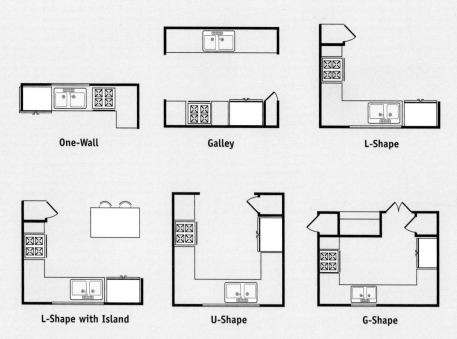

One-Wall   Galley   L-Shape

L-Shape with Island   U-Shape   G-Shape

Kitchens come in all shapes and sizes. The kitchen layout that will be most efficient and aesthetically pleasing to you—and most feasible in the space with which you have to work—depends on the dimensions of your kitchen; the basic shape the walls make; how you want your kitchen to relate to the spaces that surround it, such as the family room or dining room; and whether you want to create informal dining space within the kitchen proper.

Each layout presented here has its strong and weak points. Consider these shapes an excellent place to start: Combine and manipulate them to suit your needs.

The Work Triangle

No matter what layout you choose, keep your eye on the work triangle. This is the triangle that's formed by drawing lines from the sink to the refrigerator to the cooktop. A nice, tight work triangle is the key to an efficient kitchen. If the distance between the three features it connects is more than a few steps, you will likely tire as you rush here and there to prepare, cook, and clean.

If more than one cook will use your kitchen at the same time, plot the elements so traffic flows smoothly: You don't want one cook bumping into another as they work. Adding a second sink so each cook has his or her own area creates two triangles that intersect only at one point, for instance, the refrigerator.

In recent years, professional kitchen planners have started to talk about "work zones" and "work centers" in addition to work triangles, but the concept is the same: Keep the elements you need grouped together to avoid wasted steps, and plot traffic routes so that stoplights aren't needed to avoid collisions.

One-wall. This layout, made for smaller open spaces, is the least efficient shape because it requires one to walk up and down the stretch of wall to reach the range, refrigerator, sink, and storage. One-wall kitchens work best with a centered sink flanked by the refrigerator and cooktop, with 4 feet of counter space between each. Locate doors away from the busy work wall to avoid traffic hassles.

Galley. Many older homes have this type of long, narrow kitchen built between parallel walls. Contrary to popular belief, galley kitchens are incredibly efficient workspaces. They allow the cook to move easily with few steps between the sink, refrigerator, stove, and work spaces. Plan at least 4 feet of space between opposite counters. The best design puts the sink and refrigerator on one wall, with the cooktop centered between them on the opposite wall. Unfortunately a galley kitchen doesn't allow for much dining space, although some longer galleys successfully incorporate a breakfast nook at one end. Another downside to galleys: If doorways are located at each end of the kitchen, foot traffic crosses the work triangle, resulting in collisions. If you desire an open kitchen that has the efficiency of the galley style, build a kitchen between a wall and a length of island. That way, you can direct foot traffic to the open side of the island, which also happens to be a good place for counter dining.

1

L-shape. This layout requires two adjacent walls and is most efficient when work areas are kept close to the crook of the L. You can save footsteps by routing the work flow from refrigerator to sink to cooktop to serving areas. Because the work core tucks into a corner, traffic through the kitchen isn't a problem.

L-shape with island. Adding an island to the L-shape kitchen makes room for more than one cook and adds counter space, a place for a snack or breakfast bar, and increased space for storage and dining. The island also works as a room divider, shielding some of the kitchen clutter from adjacent spaces such as a family or dining room.

U-shape. The cozy U-shape kitchen works best when it places one workstation—the sink, cooktop, and refrigerator—on each of three walls. The U-shape kitchen is highly efficient for one cook and allows for many design possibilities, but you need at least an 8×8-foot space to make it work. Small U-shapes make

it difficult for multiple cooks to maneuver without getting in one another's way.

U-shape with island. If you're not sure how to make your large kitchen work efficiently, this layout may be the answer. You can install a sink or cooktop in the island and, if desired, a special function countertop such as marble or granite for rolling pastry. Allow at least 42 inches of aisle space to surround the island; if yours is a two-cook kitchen, 48 inches is better.

G-shape. This layout provides room for an audience. The G-shape kitchen features a peninsula anchored to a line of cabinets. You can outfit the peninsula with a cooktop or sink, enabling you to face guests while working, or you can use the peninsula as a dining bar or buffet. The peninsula also serves as a room divider, allowing family and friends to visit with the cook while remaining clear of the work area.

1 *This galley kitchen shows that space-efficient design doesn't have to come at the expense of a dark, cloistered atmosphere. By opening one end of the galley onto a window-lit dining area, the kitchen gains a sense of spaciousness, light, and connection to the rest of the house.*

2 *A gracefully arced island encloses this G-shape kitchen with a counter that's handy for serving, snacking, informal dining, or simply chatting with the cook.*

3 *L-shape-with-island kitchens such as this offer galleylike efficiency and more. The island here serves as a work space, a storage unit, a dining and serving counter, and a divider that keeps guests near, yet clear of the work core.*

Kitchen Zones

1

Zones

Interrelated centers, or zones, make your kitchen more organized, efficient, and comfortable. Just as the work triangle puts the refrigerator, sink, and cooktop within easy reach, work centers with specific functions make planning, preparing, cooking, serving, and cleaning up after a meal quick and easy. Here's an overview of the different kitchen centers and some things to keep in mind as you design them.

Planning. Reserving a space in the kitchen to plan meals, leave and collect messages, pay bills, and use a computer is a growing necessity for many homeowners. Locate the planning center well outside any work triangles so it doesn't interfere with traffic or access to storage cabinetry or appliances. If possible, include storage for books, files, a computer, and peripherals. (See Kitchen Command Centers on pages

140–141 for some inspirational examples.)

Cleanup. This center consists of the sink, garbage disposal, dishwasher, trash can or compactor, and, in many locales, a recycling bin. The sink anchors this zone and is best located in the center of the work triangle, between the range and the refrigerator. The dishwasher belongs next to the sink—to the left if the main user is right-handed and to the right if that person is left-handed. If your plans include a trash compactor, install it on the side of the sink opposite the dishwasher to save steps. The cleanup center also requires a dish draining area and ample storage for dish towels, cleaning products, and utensils.

Food storage and prep. Here's where you'll put the refrigerator, well-organized storage for canned and dry goods, mixing bowls, cook-

ware, cookbooks (if they're not stored in the planning center), and small appliances. Situate primary food storage near the longest stretch of countertop for easy access while cooking. It's best if those cabinets are attached to cool outside walls near shaded, north-facing windows and away from heat sources, such as the dishwasher or oven. If your refrigerator has one large door, place the latch-side facing into this center where the door can open completely and bins can be pulled out easily.

Cooking. The main ingredients here are the range (or cooktop and oven), its ventilation system, and a microwave. The cooking center also requires handy, accessible storage for all the tools of the cooking trade: pot holders, hot pads, spices and seasonings, and any other food products that go directly from the container into the simmering pot. If you imagined your new kitchen with a pot or utensil rack, put it here: Hanging storage keeps items close to where they're used and saves time spent rummaging through drawers to find what you need. Ideally, the cooking center should feature a heat-resistant surface near the range so you can remove hot pots from the heat without scorching the countertop. Can't find room for everything? Because baking doesn't require the close attention of stove-top cooking, consider placing ovens just outside the work triangle.

Serving and dining. Eat-in kitchens come with lots of advantages: They save steps when serving and cleaning up after a meal and provide family members and guests a place to talk, do homework, or socialize with the cook. The ideal kitchen dining area enjoys close proximity to the work core and plenty of natural light. In large kitchens,

2

the easiest way to gain dining space is to move all appliances to a corridor or L-shape layout, leaving one wall or corner for a freestanding table and chairs or a built-in banquette. In a large open kitchen, an island or peninsula with stools does the trick. Or, create a diner-style counter by cantilevering an island or peninsula work surface—an option that requires little floor space.

Specialty. If you have the space and the inclination, you can add centers designed to support other activities as well. If you're a baker, for instance, you might enjoy a baking center outfitted with a special surface for rolling dough and custom-designed storage for mixing bowls,

baking pans, small appliances, oven mitts, and ingredients. If you entertain frequently, host numerous houseguests, or just plain have a large family, a beverage center located outside the central work zones

allows people to help themselves without entering the main kitchen. Other specialized centers might serve the needs of snackers, recycling, or pet feeding.

1 *To make this cooking center as efficient as possible, an especially shallow cooktop makes way for a spice drawer directly beneath. Because a wall oven handles baking tasks in another part of the room, the space below holds pots and lids on open, slide-out trays for easy pull-and-pluck selection while cooking.*

2 *This in-kitchen dining zone bathed in natural light features a space-efficient banquette. Stored dishes, a microwave, and the dishwasher are close by, making heating, serving, and cleaning up after informal meals a snap. Paired with a shelf of cookbooks, the banquette tabletop doubles as a planning center for more formal meals.*

Designing Your Kitchen

Now that you've composed your kitchen wish list and considered the variety of kitchen configurations and work centers, you're ready to compose the design. With so many options, it can be tough getting started. Good thing there are lots of folks out there you can call on for help.

Design it yourself. Using the Kitchen Planning Kit on pages 176–181, sketch out your space, mark the location of existing features, and experiment with different options. You may well want or need to consult a professional—or even several professionals—but the exercise of working through some options yourself will help clarify your priorities before you contact a designer, architect, or contractor.

Get home center design help. Many home improvement centers employ staff who can help you lay out a kitchen at little or no charge. If you'll be working with stock cabinets and appliances, these folks often are great resources, streamlining both the design and product selection process. Keep in mind that you'll be responsible for supplying accurate measurements, and you may not receive assistance with customizing or problem solving.

Hire a kitchen designer. Kitchens are such complex rooms that an entire profession is devoted to their design. Kitchen designers combine a knowledge of interior design with an emphasis on kitchen use. They're also up-to-date on new and emerging kitchen products and technology. Certified Kitchen Designers have completed a course of study designed by the National Kitchen and Bath Association, but you'll find plenty of talent among certified and noncertified designers alike.

Consult an interior designer. Most interior designers address kitchens as well as other rooms. If you're remodeling more than your kitchen, you might choose an interior designer to assist you in pulling together the look of the entire project.

Commission an architect. Architects are especially valuable resources when you plan to make significant structural changes to your home, such as building a kitchen addition or substantially reworking its internal structure. They are often accustomed to working with interior designers and kitchen designers.

Visualization exercises

Once you have a preliminary design in hand, use these tips to visualize your new space and make the design work better for you:

Ask your architect or designer for a rendering. These three-dimensional color drawings, complete with furnishings, architectural features, and lighting sketched in, make it much easier to get a feel for the prospective space, especially if blueprints look like hieroglyphics to you.

Take a virtual tour. Your design pro also might offer to let you "tour" your project before it's constructed using a computer-aided design (CAD) program. This software lets you experiment with configurations and view the space in three dimensions from different vantage points.

Stake it out. Outline the shape and size of your reconfigured room—especially if you're working on a

[1] *This beautifully remodeled kitchen in a vintage home involved knocking down walls and annexing space from adjoining rooms. This kind of major renovation can often benefit from an architect's expertise, ensuring that the space flows well and is comfortably integrated with the rest of the house.*

major remodeling project or addition—using stakes and string in the yard. If you're considering an addition, stake it out in the proposed final location. If you're considering a kitchen that uses existing space within the house, it's still useful to stake it out; just do it where you have sufficient room (for example, in your yard, garage, or driveway). Use objects such as lawn furniture and cardboard boxes to represent a dining set, cabinetry, and appliances within the staked-out area. Walk around the "room" and see how it feels. Try to imagine using it as you would use a real kitchen. Note the locations of windows and doors as well as any views or obstacles.

Once you study the floor plan or model in conjunction with how you live day to day, you'll be able to make adjustments as necessary to create a kitchen tailored to fit.

Seamless *Additions*

If your kitchen renovation involves an addition, blend it seamlessly with the rest of the home. Details make all the difference, so pay attention to three crucial factors: roofline, proportion, and materials.

Start at the top. Make sure all roof portions mirror one another in style. Match the pitch, overhangs, soffits, fasciae, and eaves with the existing structure.

Maintain proportion. Take care that your kitchen addition won't overwhelm—or be overwhelmed by—the existing structure. It's OK for it to look like an addition, but it shouldn't look incongruous in scale.

Choose materials carefully. On the roof, match shingle style, color, and material; when using brick, match its color, size, texture, and mortar to the original. Or, complement the existing materials with something consistent with the period of the house. Windows, too, need to match, both in basic type and the details, such as muntin width and pane size. Lastly, choose a color palette in keeping with the home's period, style, and surroundings.

Kitchen Planning Kit

To transform your kitchen dreams into a reality, consider all the details. Few homeowners resist the urge to sketch out some ideas, even if they plan to work with a kitchen designer. But doing so is recommended because your drawings provide better insight into what you're after. Use the Kitchen Planning Kit on the following pages to work through the process.

To help you consider how you'll use your new kitchen, visualize the following: how traffic should flow, where you'd like the various work centers to go, how you'll work in a desk or planning area, how the kitchen relates to the rooms around it, and whether or not you'd like to incorporate a gathering, snacking, or dining area into the room. Finally, consider which architectural features you'd like to add or highlight and what types, sizes, and styles of appliances, cabinetry, shelving, and furnishings you want to include.

Plot the space using the grids on pages 180–181 (1 square equals 1 square foot of floor space). Plot your kitchen, including any pantry, entry, mudroom, office, dining area, or bump-outs you'd like to add or remodel at the same time. One of the keys to making your kitchen both functional and beautiful is good placement of doors, windows, appliances, cabinetry, islands, and built-in features.

Use the architectural symbols below to mark the position of existing architectural features. Use a different color to indicate added features such as the placement of built-ins and furniture. Use dotted lines to mark obstructions, including prominent light fixtures and angled ceilings.

Use the templates to experiment with different placements for furniture, appliances, and built-in features. Trace or photocopy the appropriate items from the templates on the following pages and cut them out with a crafts knife or scissors. If you have furniture or special features such as a peninsula or island, measure and draw them to the same scale (1 square equals 1 square foot) on the grid paper.

Find or create a focal point. Each room needs a focal point, a cornerstone around which to build the room's design. The focal point is the dramatic element that draws you into the room. If your kitchen doesn't have an existing focal point, consider adding one: a dramatic window, a center island, a boldly colored or styled appliance, or large artwork.

Architectural Symbols:

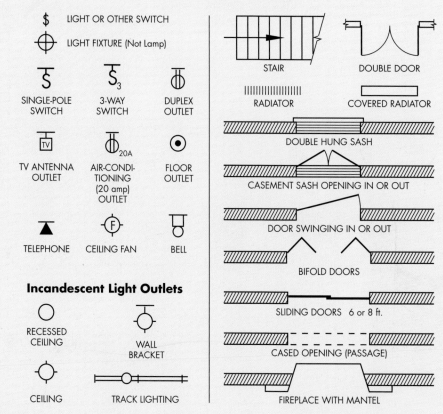

$ LIGHT OR OTHER SWITCH

LIGHT FIXTURE (Not Lamp)

SINGLE-POLE SWITCH

3-WAY SWITCH

DUPLEX OUTLET

TV ANTENNA OUTLET

AIR-CONDITIONING (20 amp) OUTLET

FLOOR OUTLET

TELEPHONE

CEILING FAN

BELL

Incandescent Light Outlets

RECESSED CEILING

WALL BRACKET

CEILING

TRACK LIGHTING

STAIR

DOUBLE DOOR

RADIATOR

COVERED RADIATOR

DOUBLE HUNG SASH

CASEMENT SASH OPENING IN OR OUT

DOOR SWINGING IN OR OUT

BIFOLD DOORS

SLIDING DOORS   6 or 8 ft.

CASED OPENING (PASSAGE)

FIREPLACE WITH MANTEL

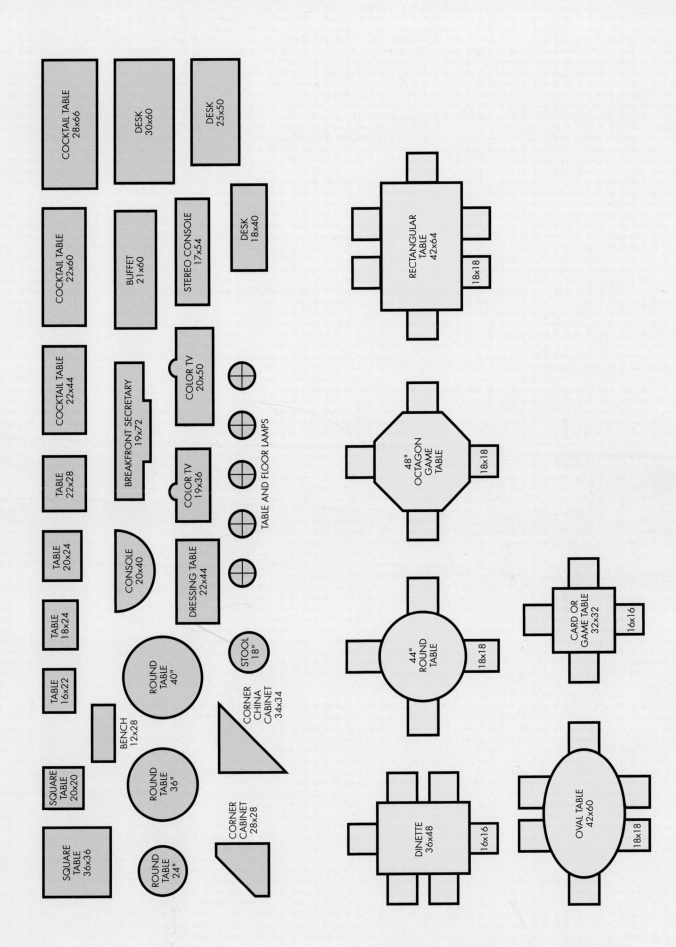

COCKTAIL TABLE
28x66

DESK
30x60

DESK
25x50

COCKTAIL TABLE
22x60

BUFFET
21x60

STEREO CONSOLE
17x54

DESK
18x40

COCKTAIL TABLE
22x44

TABLE
22x28

TABLE
20x24

TABLE
18x24

TABLE
16x22

SQUARE TABLE
20x20

SQUARE TABLE
36x36

BREAKFRONT SECRETARY
19x72

COLOR TV
20x50

COLOR TV
19x36

CONSOLE
20x40

DRESSING TABLE
22x44

ROUND TABLE
40"

ROUND TABLE
36"

ROUND TABLE
24"

BENCH
12x28

STOOL
18"

CORNER CHINA CABINET
34x34

CORNER CABINET
28x28

TABLE AND FLOOR LAMPS

RECTANGULAR TABLE
42x64
18x18

48" OCTAGON GAME TABLE
18x18

44" ROUND TABLE
18x18

CARD OR GAME TABLE
32x32
16x16

DINETTE
36x48
16x16

OVAL TABLE
42x60
18x18

177

Kitchen Planning Kit

Base Cabinets

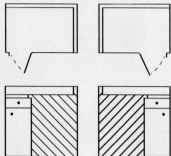

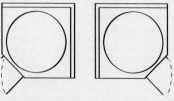

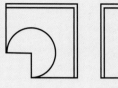

Blind Corner

Lazy Susan Angle

Lazy Susan Corner

Cabinetry

9" Tray	12"	15"	18"	21"	24"	27"	30"	33"	36"

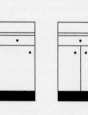

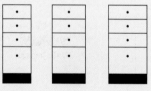

Sink Bases

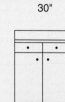

36"	48"	30"

Template *Time*

Use these templates to mark the placement of common kitchen components. The templates include both plan-view ("top-down") and elevation ("side view") perspectives, allowing you to create both floor plans and wall elevations. Most kitchen components are represented here, including various types and sizes of drop-in and freestanding ranges, cooktops, grills, and refrigerators. Pay attention to details like door swings and drawer extensions (marked in dotted lines on these templates) as you consider the placement of these items in the room. If you don't see a template for something you'd like to include, draw your own.

Appliances

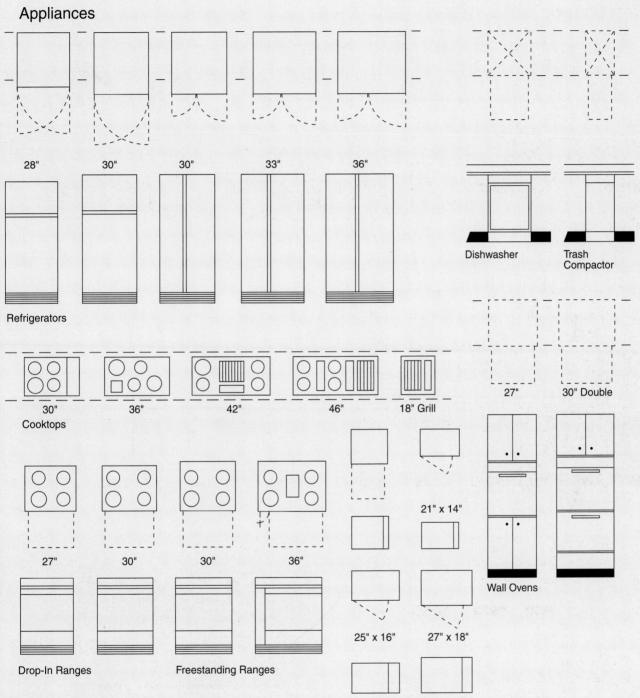

28" 30" 30" 33" 36"

Refrigerators

Dishwasher

Trash Compactor

Cooktops

30" 36" 42" 46" 18" Grill

27" 30" Double

27" 30" 30" 36"

Drop-In Ranges Freestanding Ranges

21" x 14"

25" x 16" 27" x 18"

Wall Ovens

Microwave Ovens

Planning Grid

Use a photocopier to reproduce the grid at its original size, then cut out the templates on pages 177–179 to design your new or remodeled kitchen. Grid scale: 1 square equals 1 square foot.

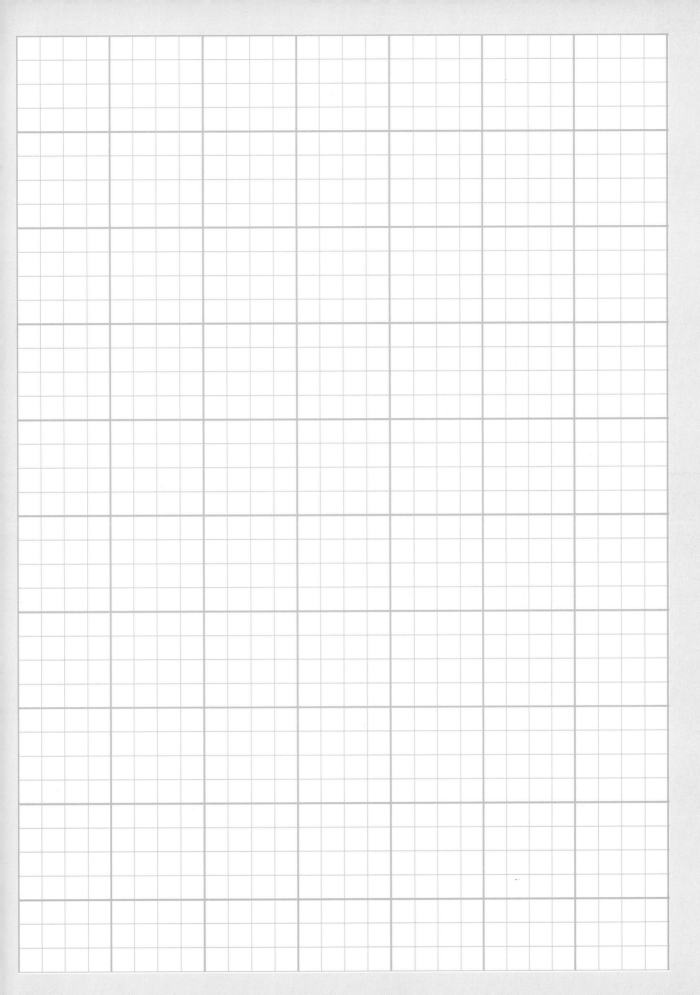

Selecting a Pro

Choosing the best professionals to design and build your project makes the entire experience more enjoyable and ensures top-notch results. Whether you're searching for a kitchen designer, architect, or contractor, use the following tactics to track down the best one for you.

Gather. Collect the names of professionals to investigate and interview. Ask friends and colleagues for recommendations. Identify local referrals with the help of professional organizations such as the American Institute of Architects (800-242-3837, www.aia.org), The National Kitchen and Bath Association (877-NKBA-PRO, www.nkba.org), and The National Association of Home Builders Remodelors Council (800-368-5242 ext. 8216, www.nahb.org).

Explore. Select four to six individuals from each of the professions you plan to use. Call the architects, kitchen designers, interior designers, and remodeling contractors on your list and ask for references. Then contact those references and ask them to recount their positive and negative experiences. If you come across a recent remodeling project that you like, contact the homeowners to find out who did it and ask about their experience.

Evaluate. Based on these references, interview the top three candidates in each profession and tour some of their finished projects. Savvy architects, designers, and contractors will ask you questions as well to determine your expectations and needs. You should come away from each interview and tour with a feel for the quality of that professional's work and how well your personalities and visions for the project mesh.

Solicit. To narrow your choices between two or more architects or kitchen designers, it may be worth the additional cost to solicit preliminary drawings from each one. This is a great way to test your working relationship. Also, ask contractors for bids, but don't base your decision on cost alone. Instead weigh what you learned in the interview with the thoroughness of the bid itself.

Sign up. Before hiring a professional for any project, write up a contract that legally protects you before, during, and after the work is done. Define the scope of the project and fees as specifically as possible. Include a clear description of the work to be done, materials required, and who will supply them. In addition, spell out commencement and completion dates and any provisions relating to timelines. Include your

---

Stages and Phases

Prepare for your kitchen project by knowing what to expect during the process and how to save money. While no two kitchen projects are exactly alike, they normally follow a process similar to the following.

Plan. During this stage, determine whether you'll use a design professional. Either way, you'll need to pin down the design and begin shaping the budget. When shopping for elements, find out how long it will take to receive building and surface materials and appliances once they are ordered; figure this into the project completion schedule. Once your design is complete, select a contractor. Note that some contractors may suggest alternatives for accomplishing some aspects of the design. Before moving to the next stage, finish the budget and determine a timeline. This is also a good time to select products and arrange for delivery.

Confer. Invite the key players—the architect or designer, the contractor, primary subcontractors, and the job supervisor—to your home. Tour your kitchen together and review the project particulars. This is also a good time to establish any ground rules—including those that concern communication—between you and the professionals you hire. One idea is to place a notebook in a prominent location where both you and the crew can jot down comments and questions.

Prepare. Remove your personal belongings from the job site. To prevent dust and debris from spreading throughout the house, hang plastic sheeting and seal it securely between the job site and the rest of the house.

Demolish. Remove any built-in structures such as cabinetry, counters, islands, or walls that will not be included in the final project during this stage. Doing the demolition yourself may save you money. If that's an option you'd like to explore, discuss your participation with your contractor during the Plan and Confer stages.

Construct. Here's where the project all comes together. If you're building an addition, the foundation and framing go up first. Next come windows, plumbing, electrical wiring, and heating, ventilation, and air-conditioning ductwork, followed by insulation, drywall, roofing, and siding. Finish carpentry and electrical connections are next, then the flooring. After that, appliances, light fixtures, and plumbing fixtures are installed. Wood floors can be sanded, stained, and sealed at this stage.

Finish. Walk through the completed project with your contractor and architect, noting any concerns or unfinished details. It's the contractor's responsibility to follow up on your list and complete the project.

1

1 The beautiful design, elegant material choices, and faultless workmanship in this high-end kitchen are the result of a well-chosen design-and-build team. Interview several before settling on those candidates you'd like to use. Then request bids and check references before signing anyone on.

total costs (subject to additions and deductions by a written change order only), and tie payments to work stages. Be wary of any contractor who asks for a lot of money up front. If certain materials need to be ordered weeks in advance (to allow for manufacturing), get a list of those materials and their costs before making a down payment. Kitchens usually require a sizable cash advance to finance appliances and cabinetry.

Funding Sources

Kitchen redos aren't cheap—the average job costs about $20,000, according to the National Association of Home Builders Remodelor's Council. Fortunately there are many ways to pay.

With savings. If you've socked away enough to fund your project, you're sitting pretty: no waiting, no finance costs, no payments to make.

With income. By doing a major project in stages, you can pay for (and complete) a portion of the work over a set period of time. This is another way to avoid finance costs. By stretching out the project, you also buy time to shop for bargains on big-ticket elements, such as appliances and cabinetry, and to do some or all of the work yourself. On the other hand, it prolongs the inconvenience of not having a kitchen, and if you end up dining out during that time, you may literally eat up any savings you accrue.

With a home equity loan. If you have enough equity in your home to pay for the kitchen you want, you may be able to finance the project with a lump-sum home equity loan. If you don't have enough savings to fund your project and you don't like the inconvenience of paying as you go, a home equity loan is an attractive alternative. They're often tax deductible and rates are generally lower than for consumer loans.

With a home equity line of credit. A home equity line of credit is a loan that allows you to borrow up to a preset amount on a revolving credit account that works similarly to a credit card, yet generally with lower rates and tax-deductible interest. The advantage over the lump-sum loan is that you only pay interest on money as you spend it. Because the cost of a renovation is spread over time as you buy materials and pay contractors, the interest costs for a line of credit will be less than that of a lump-sum loan, all other factors being equal.

With a mortgage. If you're planning to remodel a home that you're about to buy, ask your lender about the possibility of getting a mortgage for the price of the home plus the price of the kitchen you desire. The interest you pay is tax-deductible, and the cost will be spread out over the term of the loan, making this a relatively painless and money-savvy option.

With a credit card. Due to credit cards' high interest rates, use this source of funding only as a last resort. However, in some cases this method is useful if—for example, you're taking advantage of a low "teaser" interest rate, need to borrow a relatively small amount, and/or can pay off your balance quickly. Be careful, though, because a combination of cost overruns, job delays, and teaser-rate expiration dates can leave you with a big, high-interest balance to pay.

With a combination of sources. Sometimes a patchwork of funding from a variety of sources is the way to go: You might have some savings, pay some as you go, purchase appliances with a special no-interest-for-a-year retailer's promotion, and contribute some of your own sweat equity to the project.

Remodeling Survival Tips To ensure that the inconveniences of a remodeling project don't turn into major headaches, discuss your concerns with your contractor before work begins. At your preconstruction meeting (where you, the contractor, and the construction manager are present), ask for an overview of the entire construction process and develop a plan to minimize disruption to the household.

• Discuss what the contractor will do to control dust. Most contractors tape a plastic barrier over doorways to reduce the amount of dust that escapes from the construction zone. Some also may tape off heat registers and change furnace filters daily, especially when sanding drywall.

• Request floor protection. Request that walkways and carpeted areas that lead to the construction zone be covered with drop cloths or plastic runners.

• Realize that noise is inevitable. Ask workers to arrive and leave at reasonable hours but understand that if you set shorter workdays, you may lengthen the duration of the project.

• Coordinate schedules. Let the contractor know in advance if there are any times, such as holidays or special family events, when your house will be off-limits to project work.

• Set up camp. Make temporary changes to minimize disruption and inconvenience. Move the refrigerator, the coffeepot, and the microwave to the dining room to reduce problems that come with limited accessibility.

1 *High-quality kitchens like this one cost money. Fortunately you have a variety of financing options, some of which offer tax advantages depending upon your situation.*

Controlling Costs

Work around objects that are costly to move, such as plumbing stacks, heat runs, and chimneys. You'll reduce costs if you leave exterior openings (for instance doors, windows, chimneys, plumbing stacks, and kitchen vent fans) in their original locations.

Doing It Yourself

If you enjoy working with tools and have a basic knowledge of home construction, you might consider remodeling your kitchen yourself. The homeowner featured here took time off work to gut and remodel her own kitchen, calling on a pro only to assist her with gas line installation. She estimates that doing the work herself saved about $10,000. Here are some tips to help you get the best results from your efforts:

If your plans and projects are bigger than your billfold, use the following tips to help save money.

Choose materials wisely. Birch cabinets cost two to three times less than solid cherry, and you can personalize them with stains, paint, or stenciling. Another trick is to buy stock cabinets and customize them with molding.

Get help. Swap jobs with handy neighbors. Throw a party and feed guests in exchange for some labor. Ask family and friends to help out.

Assist as a general laborer. Consider tackling simple grading, tearing up carpet, wallpapering, painting, and minor trim work and cleanup. A cost-plus-fixed-fee contract credits your labor against a contractor's fee.

Act as your own contractor. This is a full-time job and not a task for the faint of heart. You need to understand the project, the order of work, and have a thorough knowledge of building codes.

Rent the equipment needed if you're completing part of the project yourself. Buying equipment usually costs more.

Compare prices. Your contractor gets a discount on many products, but you might pay less if you shop around and buy your own materials.

Keep the shape simple if you're building an addition. A square foundation costs less than one with lots of angles. To add interest inside, angle interior walls, leave ceilings open to the roofline, and pay attention to finish details such as molding.

1 *It isn't that hard.* This homeowner learned everything she knows about wiring at the library. She reads up on tasks such as installing electrical outlets before she begins her project.

2 *Review all your options.* Some products designed for quick-and-easy do-it-yourself use actually cost more than upscale materials. These high-quality ceramic tiles cost significantly less, for instance, then peel-and-stick vinyl tiles. Although installation involved mixing grout and renting a tile saw, it was easier than laying the vinyl tiles because the smoothness of the underlayment wasn't nearly as critical or time-consuming. The result is a far more durable floor.

3 *Get creative.* Working on a project yourself allows you to add custom features to suit your own aesthetic—often at less cost than having something run-of-the-mill professionally installed. This homeowner chose to create a backsplash with polished stones set in the same grout used to lay

the tile floor. The result is a unique, gem-like look.

4 **Set up an outdoor work area.** *Use a porch, patio, or driveway to complete dusty operations. In this case, the homeowner used a deck off the kitchen as a handy spot for doing messy work such as cutting tile backer-board. In most cases, you won't need a shop: New lightweight, easy-to-use tools such as this rotary saw equipped with a cutting wheel make easy work of jobs that used to require heavy, expensive professional tools.*

5 **Measure twice, cut once.** *That old carpenter's adage is important when dealing with stock materials such as tile backer-board. It's even more crucial when ordering custom or made-to-measure countertops or cabinetry. But if you can sew, frame a picture, or build a simple bookshelf, you already have the basic measuring skills you need to ensure your materials will cut to a perfect fit.*

Resources

Consult the following organizations, books, magazines, and websites for additional kitchen design and planning information—and inspiration.

Organizations
• **The National Association of Home Builders**
800-368-5242
www.nahb.org
This industry site offers information for consumers to learn more about the home building and remodeling process, from hiring professionals, financing, and contracts to insurance and surviving the process.
• **The National Kitchen and Bath Association**
877-NKBA-PRO
www.nkba.org
Turn to this site to find a design professional in your area and information on industry trends, products, and services. You can request a free consumer workbook, browse designers' answers to common kitchen-related questions, read articles on numerous aspects of kitchen design, and view award-winning kitchens.

Building Codes and Building Officials
Building codes are designed to protect the structural integrity of your home, safeguarding your health and safety and that of your family, friends, and anyone who comes in contact with your home. Before you plan a remodeling project, visit the local building department; doing so will help you take your ideas further and may well be one of the most enlightening 15 minutes you invest in your project.

Your governing building official and codes will likely be the building department of your town or city government. If you live outside city limits, this function may be performed at the county level by a clerk or commission. Occasionally county officials don't govern a property, and you'll need to call the state departments of building standards or housing to find a governing official.

Be prepared to tell the officials what you're thinking of doing, even if your ideas are rough, and ask them what building codes will apply. A rough sketch of the available space and the location of windows, doors, and mechanical systems will make your visit even more productive. Don't be dissuaded if local codes call for a standard that you can't meet. Ask about exceptions: Many officials are willing to make them to accommodate existing buildings if safety or practicality isn't compromised.

Better Homes and Gardens® Online Resources
Visit the *Better Homes and Gardens* website at www.bhg.com, where you'll find a wealth of ideas and help. Special features on the site include the following:
• **Arrange-a-Room** Try this interactive tool that allows you to lay out any room in your home.
• **The BHG.com/Home Improvement Encyclopedia**
Go to this page for help with interior and exterior improvement, repair projects and updates, information on do-it-yourself projects, calculators to help you estimate costs and materials, and a tool dictionary.
• **Decorating Center** From design lessons to projects and ideas, you'll

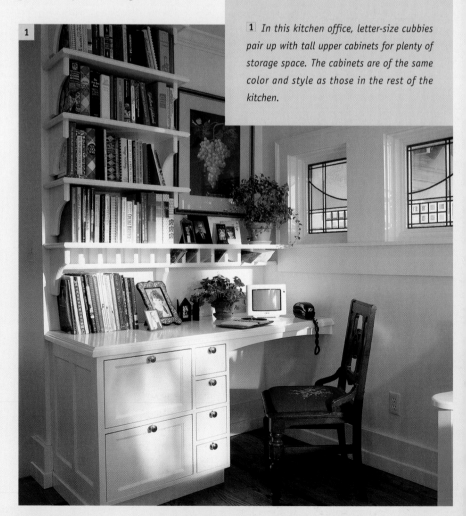

1 *In this kitchen office, letter-size cubbies pair up with tall upper cabinets for plenty of storage space. The cabinets are of the same color and style as those in the rest of the kitchen.*

find the information you want here.

• **Home Solutions** Turn here for everything from quick fixes to remodeling project ideas.

• **Painting Center** Click on this page to find painting projects, ideas, and help with interior, exterior, and decorative painting techniques and color choices.

• **Ready, Set, Organize** Find efficient, inspired storage ideas here.

Books and Magazines

The following *Better Homes and Gardens®* publications are available on newsstands and in bookstores. Or, order them online at www.bhgbooks.com.

• **Books**
  • *Complete Kitchens*
  • *Exterior Style Planner*
  • *Kitchen Planner*
  • *Kitchens*
  • *Remodeling Idea File*
  • *Step-by-Step Kitchen and Bath Projects*
• **Magazines**
  • *Better Homes and Gardens*
  • *Country Home*
  • *Kitchen & Bath Ideas*
  • *Kitchen & Bath Products Guide*
  • *Kitchen Planning Guide*
  • *Remodeling Ideas*
  • *Remodeling Products Guide*
  • *Renovation Style*
  • *Traditional Home*
  • *Traditional Home Decorator Showcase*

Manufacturer Resources and Online Tools

These online and interactive design tools allow you to fine-tune your remodeling ideas. Some sites allow you to drop product choices into room style settings, then change the color of the walls and features to preview various combinations. Other sites feature extensive "galleries" of ideas. Use these sites to get started. Or, call the manufacturers directly to find what products are available in your area.

Appliances

• Amana Appliances
800-843-0304
www.amana.com

• Dacor
800-793-0093
www.dacor.com
• DCS (Dynamic Cooking Systems, Inc.)
800-433-8466
www.dcsappliances.com
• Fisher & Paykel Appliances, Inc.
800-863-5384
www.fisherpaykel.com
• Frigidaire Home Products
800-444-4944
www.frigidaire.com
• GE Appliances
800-626-2000
www.geappliances.com
• Jenn-Air
800-536-6247
www.jennair.com
• Kenmore, by Sears
888-536-6673
www.kenmore.com
• KitchenAid
800-422-1230
www.kitchenaid.com
• Sub-Zero
800-222-7820
www.subzero.com
• Thermador
800-656-9226
www.thermador.com
• Viking Range Corp.
888-845-4641
www.vikingrange.com

Cabinetry

• KraftMaid Cabinetry
800-654-3008
www.kraftmaid.com
• Merillat Industries
www.merillat.com
• Plain & Fancy Custom Cabinetry
800-447-9006
www.plainfancycabinetry.com

Resources

- Rutt Custom Cabinetry, LLC
800-420-7888
www.rutt1.com
- SieMatic
800-765-5266

Flooring
- Armstrong Floors
www.armstrongfloors.com
- Congoleum Floors
www.congoleum.com

Sinks and Faucets
- Delta Faucet Company
www.deltafaucet.com
- Elkay
630-572-3192
www.elkay.com
- Kohler
800-456-4537
www.kohler.com
- Moen
800-BUY-MOEN
www.moen.com

Window Manufacturers
- Anderson Windows
www.andersonwindows.com
- Hy-Lite Products (glass block)
www.hy-lite.com
- Pella Windows
www.pella.com
- Pozzi Wood Windows
www.pozzi.com
- Velux-America (skylights)
www.velux-america.com
- Weathershield Windows
www.weathershield.com

Acknowledgments
Fresh Dress stylist, pages 67–69: Becky Jerdee.
Photography courtesy of the following Meredith publications: *Better Homes and Gardens*® magazine, *Better Homes and Gardens® Beautiful Kitchens* magazine, *Better Homes and Gardens® Do It Yourself* magazine, *Better Homes and Gardens® Kitchen and Bath Ideas* magazine, *Better Homes and Gardens® Kitchen and Bath Products Guide* magazine, *Better Homes and Gardens® Kitchen Planning Guide* magazine, *Better Homes and Gardens® Quick and Easy Decorating* magazine, *Better Homes and Gardens® Remodeling Ideas* magazine, *Better Homes and Gardens® Remodeling Planning Guide* magazine, *Better Homes and Gardens® Remodeling Planning & Products Guide* magazine, *Renovation Style*® magazine, *Traditional Home*® magazine, *Traditional Home® Decorators' Showhouse* magazine.

Index

Index